Human(e)

A radical reimagining of grief, loss, and learning to live without

Rachelle Bensoussan

DEMETER

Human(e)
A radical reimagining of grief, loss, and learning to live without
Rachelle Bensoussan

Demeter Press
PO Box 197
Coe Hill, Ontario
Canada
K0L 1P0
Tel: 289-383-0134
Email: info@demeterpress.org
Website: www.demeterpress.org

Demeter Press logo based on the sculpture "Demeter" by Maria-Luise Bodirsky
www.keramik-atelier.bodirsky.de

Printed and Bound in Canada

Cover design: Matthew Watson and Stacy de la Rosa
Typesetting: Michelle Pirovich
Proof reading: Jena Woodhouse

Library and Archives Canada Cataloguing in Publication
Title: Human(e): a radical reimagining of grief, loss and learning to live without / by Rachelle Bensoussan.
Other titles: Human
Names: Bensoussan, Rachelle, author.
Description: Includes bibliographical references.
Identifiers: Canadiana 20240412451 | ISBN 9781772585049 (softcover)
Subjects: LCSH: Bensoussan, Rachelle. | LCSH: Grief. | LCSH: Grief—Social aspects. | LCGFT: Autobiographies.
Classification: LCC BF575.G7 B46 2024 | DDC 152.4—dc23

Funded by the Government of Canada | Canada

The publisher gratefully acknowledges the support of the Government of Canada

For Di.

And for all of you,
the ones who remain.

Contents

i have loved you like
the soles of shoes worn in every country.
like the back of my hand.
like the inside of my eyelids.
like a breath. like every breath.
—Alison Malee

Prologue

Sometimes the hardest thing is simply to begin. This book began eighteen years ago on November 29, 2005. That was the night the woman I loved most in the world died. It was the night that I did, too. Allow me to share with you this unspoken secret of the bereaved: the living continue on long after the person, and the world, they once recognized as their own are lost forever.

I am starting this book in a place far from where the original story began. I am in a different country and time zone. The language spoken is not my own, and the faces do not resemble mine. Yet the worn, aged look of the buildings, the way construction begins but never quite completes, the garbage strewn bare in the hot sun, and the orphaned animals who roam free, all resemble so much of what has become of me in the years that have passed since her death. The night she died, she left me with a singular, irrefutable truth: we will all die broken and incomplete, and yet, this messy, painful, beautiful thing we call life is so much more than its unfinished ending. As was she.

So much life has happened since that cold November night. I write this now married to another equally unapologetic, blue-eyed woman. I have a daughter, who despite her North African and Middle Eastern ancestry, burst into the world with the same red hair and blue eyes as the woman I loved, and buried, long before she was even an idea. She emerged with my grandfather's face, as if all those who loved her from wherever it is we come, had loved her into being, infusing her with parts of themselves so I would always be able to see them and remember them when I look at her face. How ridiculous of them to think I would ever, could ever, forget.

When I was in the fifth grade, one of my classmates landed the role of

Young Cosette in the Canadian Stage production of *Les Misérables.* The night I went to see her perform was my first introduction to musical theatre. It was a night that would change the course of my life forever. From the moment I learned that you could sing for a living, I was sold. Singing and being on Broadway became my singular focus. I was a theatre nerd in every possible sense of the word. I knew the words to every major Broadway musical. I listened (and sang along) to musical theatre constantly. I sang in the shower. I sang in the car. I sang when I didn't even know I was singing.

After years of singing lessons, at the age of seventeen, I moved to Toronto to pursue an undergraduate fine arts degree in theatre. I did my final year of university abroad studying theatre and voice in Newcastle, England, and when I returned, I quickly moved to New York City to begin a summer musical theatre program at NYU. At the age of twenty-two, I was living and studying in New York City, seeing Broadway shows weekly, and was certain my wildest dreams lay just around the bend.

Are you familiar with the saying, "Life is what happens to you while you're busy making other plans?" As I was busy making plans, life showed up in the form of a petite, red-headed, blue-eyed, classically trained singer named Diane. Diane, or Di, as everyone called her, had had perfect pitch since the age of four. She was a member of the Canadian Opera Company and had understudied the role of Christine in the Toronto production of *Phantom of the Opera*. Although Shakespeare wrote the infamous lines—"Though she be but little she is fierce"—in 1595, centuries before she was born, I know he could only have had her in mind when he wrote them. I loved her instantly. The only thing equal to my love of Di was my fear. She was fiery, passionate, and packed a solid amount of intimidation into her petite frame. When we would sing together, she would yell at me fervidly, being sure to point how my vowels lacked boundaries. When our mutual friend Emily, another stunning singer, performed in front of her, Di quickly and directly said, "Is there something important you'd like to say, or do you just want to keep standing there looking and sounding pretty?" She was not known to mince words. What remains undeniable is that underneath every sharp critique was an enormous amount of care and regard. More than that, there was belief. Di believed in me more than any other human I have ever encountered. "Finish strong, Rachelle," she would say. "Finish strong." I could not have known then the significance those words would have, as I later faced the sickening likelihood of existing in a world without her.

It was early in 2005 when Di started complaining of back pain. One of her oldest and dearest friends was a chiropractor and she began seeing her for treatments. She assumed it was a strained muscle from running or something similar. Despite her attempts at acupuncture and massage the pain only increased, so much so that by the middle of March, she was having to cancel some of her work commitments due to pain and immobility. In April, Di visited her family doctor for her annual physical, and the doctor noticed a suspicious mole on her body. He said he would like to have it biopsied and asked if she was having any other symptoms or pain. She shared with him the troubles she was having with her back but assumed the two were largely unrelated. When the biopsy came back malignant for melanoma, the most serious form of skin cancer, he sent her for an MRI. It was then, in May of 2005, that we learned she had stage IV metastatic melanoma. The pain in her back was from a tumour that was engulfing her spine. The cancer had spread to every major part of her body apart from her neck and brain. They estimated it would take anywhere from three to six months to do so. Despite numerous rounds of chemotherapy, two clinical trials and an experimental treatment in Buffalo, New York, Diane died on Tuesday, November 29, 2005, at 9:45 p.m.

Many singers will tell you that singing is simply breathing on pitch. To sing is to breathe. One cannot occur without the other. For years after Diane died, whenever I would take a long, deep breath, my throat would tighten, and hot tears would spring to my eyes. I couldn't take a solid, deep breath without being entirely overcome with grief. As you can imagine, this was not great for a singer. In many ways, my dream of being on Broadway died with her on that dark November night. People always say that life can change in an instant, but it is something else altogether when it is *your* life that suddenly vanishes. In the blink of an eye, the things I had valued most in the world became meaningless. It was like trying to put on a pair of pants that simply did not fit. I was like Cinderella's stepsisters trying to force myself into the life I once called my own.

I remember going to an audition a few months after she died. It was a commercial audition for a light version of a popular candy bar. In the commercial, a woman was to open the drawer to her office desk, and the candy bar was to float up because it was so light. She was then supposed to try and catch the candy bar. In the audition, we were to pretend that we saw the candy bar floating up in front of us and mimic the actions of catching it. The director said action, and as I opened the office drawer, I looked up with tears streaming down my face and sobbed, "This is so dumb. None of this matters. You could train a monkey to do this." Needless to say, I didn't land the job.

I flailed for years after she died. I didn't know who I was without her, without singing, without music. I was lost, and I was completely unrecognizable to myself. The pain of her absence, of her death, brought me to my knees. It was suffocating. Every bit of life served only to remind me of the one she had lost.

One of the compounding factors to my grief was the age I was when she died. She died less than six weeks after my twenty-fifth birthday. At the time, I did not have any peers who had experienced something similar, and my age seemed to give those around me ample permission to share both tactless and unsolicited advice. I was constantly told how lucky I was to be so young. People seemed compelled to remind me of how much life I had ahead of me to look forward to. I was told by one particular acquaintance that I must be so relieved this ordeal was over so that I could return to New York City and resume my life. My own father told me that I should be happy for her that her suffering was over and that I should stop wallowing in her death. He shared this particular bit of wisdom with me the day before I buried her. Of the hundreds of emotions I was experiencing daily, lucky, relieved, and happy were decidedly not amongst them.

I became obsessed with grief. I wanted to learn and read every last thing I could on the subject. The experience of it was so vastly different to what I had been taught to believe it would be like. Why was no one telling the truth? How had this universally human phenomenon been both silenced and so grievously misrepresented? Grief become my new singular focus. I travelled through West Africa and the Middle East meeting others my age who had experienced significant loss. I volunteered at a camp in the Californian desert for children with life-limiting medical conditions. I was fascinated by the parts of grief that seemed universal versus the parts that seemed entirely influenced by culture, class, and access. Finally, two years after her death, I applied to graduate school to get my master's degree in thanatology. Thanatology is the scientific study of death, dying, and the losses incurred as a result. It also investigates the mechanisms and forensic aspects of death, such as bodily changes and the postmortem period, as well as the wider psychological and social aspects related to death, dying, grief and loss. And so it was in the fall of 2007, on a beautiful college campus in the mid-Atlantic state of Maryland, that I took my first official step away from Broadway and walked forward into the unknown.

Grief Literacy

A Brief History

I coined the term "grief literacy" in 2014 in response to a repeated occurrence I was witnessing in my professional world. Over and over again, I witnessed physicians, nurses, social workers, and mental health practitioners step in to support those who were grieving without ever having received any formal, mandated grief and loss education or training themselves. I witnessed the most harmful myths and misconceptions about grief and loss being shared as though they were definitive truths. I witnessed people's unexamined beliefs and biases about grief being shared as though they were clinical, evidence-based facts. I witnessed human beings at their most vulnerable soak in these unsubstantiated claims as though they were a vetted collection of professional expertise. I understood that what bereaved folks needed most was not the counsel and interference of untrained professionals but rather an accurate, pragmatic, and experience-based handbook that could offer them a roadmap for what they were experiencing. What was missing and needed was literacy: grief literacy.

Literacy is competence or knowledge in a specified area. I began to refer to my body of work and my non-pathology-based orientation of grief and loss as grief literacy—a rejection of the long-held, long-standing belief that grief requires professional intervention. It was a way of reclaiming the inherent knowledge that has been deliberately and systemically taken from us. It was a way of calling into question the enormous amount of authority and power that has been bestowed upon these so-called professionals and offering it back to those with the true expertise: the bereaved.

It has been over a decade since I coined this term and began sharing it publicly at conferences and speaking engagements across the United States and Canada. Since that time, many professionals have taken the term and claimed it as their own. Many of them have done so after sitting in the very rooms I was presenting in; one was even so bold as to publish a journal article claiming she and her colleagues coined the term themselves just a few short months after having sat on a panel with me in 2018 where I presented my work on the subject. Of course, when this happens, not only are the origins of the term excluded, but the term itself is often co-opted and taken so far out of its original context that it is no longer recognizable. The great irony being that this term, which was originally created by the bereaved and for the bereaved, is now being used by professionals to try and legitimize their own efficacy. Although I cannot officially trademark generic words or phrases, my hope is that you will not separate the language of grief literacy from the context and community from which it was born. It was—and will always be—a term that belongs to us: the ones who remain.

Before We Begin

Despite each of us having our own intersections of identity (for example, I am a Queer woman of North African and Middle Eastern descent who lives with an invisible disability), we all still navigate and live within larger systems that often have harmful and oppressive repercussions on our daily lives. Some of these larger systems that we continue to be impacted by, regardless of our own personal identities, include the patriarchy, capitalism, white supremacy, colonialism, ableism, classism, racism, and heteronormativity. For the purpose of this book, anytime I refer to our "culture" or use the term "we," I am referring to these larger systems rather than to any one of our own individual lived experiences or identities. This is important to note because in no way would I ever want to erase any of our own deeply unique and diverse individual lived experiences of grief and loss; however, I do want to explore how larger systems, and the cultures they create, influence our experiences of grief and loss. For example, Mohawk people participate in a variety of mourning rituals that take place over a ten-day period. Here in Ontario, employees are only offered three days of paid bereavement leave for the death of an immediate family member. Should a Mohawk person want to participate in their culture's traditional mourning rituals, they will have to absorb the financial cost of taking time off unpaid or risk losing their job, therefore foregoing their traditional ways of mourning. This is just one example of how the systems we inhabit can negatively influence someone's individual experience of grief and loss. When our culture denies people access to their traditional and innate ways of mourning, we impede their ability to metabolize their grief and cause unnecessary harm.

yes
i learned to live without you.

no
i did not
want to.

—Ben Maxfield

Introduction

The hospice palliative care sector in Ontario has long been a frighteningly homogenous scene. Not only in my place of work but also at conferences and events within the field, I was often one of very few, if not the only, to hold intersecting identities of marginalization. I am a Queer woman of North African and Middle Eastern descent. My grandmother was born in Rabat, Morocco, and my father in the Middle East. I come from a long line of displaced and exiled people—strangers in foreign lands. As such, it perhaps was inevitable that I would find myself an outsider as I moved through the world of hospice palliative care in Canada. It was not an uncommon experience throughout my career to be scapegoated as the problem employee or the angry, man-hating lesbian when pointing out instances of discrimination in the workplace. When a white coworker of mine dressed up as Michael Jackson for Halloween, I was the one disciplined for making her feel shamed when I addressed it. On another occasion, I was disciplined by my then-executive director for disrespecting her religious beliefs when I suggested there might be other holidays outside of Christmas to recognize and celebrate. Repeatedly I was told both implicitly and explicitly that the feelings of my white colleagues were more important than the harm being done to BIPOC and 2SLGBTQIA+ families, more important than the harm that was being done to me.

Hospices are primarily volunteer run. This is because the federal government of Canada only funds 60 per cent of clinical services associated with residential hospices in Ontario. This means that it is up to the hospice itself to fundraise the additional 40 per cent of clinical costs along with all other operational costs. A tremendous amount of money needs to be raised each year to keep the doors open. This is where volunteers come in. More than any other sector, volunteers in hospice provide much of the required day-to-day labour and care. They answer phones, cook, serve meals, offer support to the dying and their families, host and staff fundraising events, sit on the board of directors, etc. The gifts they bring are boundless. Where this can become problematic is that volunteers as a demographic are somewhat self-selecting, meaning that not all people have the time, resources, or capacity to volunteer. Those who do are often well resourced and make up a largely homogenous group. When your entire donor and labour base is made up of volunteers, they—in addition to their beliefs and biases—hold a tremendous amount of power and influence.

Over the course of my career, I came to notice two things that unbeknownst to me would become the foundational pillars of my work. The first thing I noticed was the disconnect between what was being said and what was being practiced. Across the hospice palliative care sector, there is a professional consensus that grief is normal. If you asked them, most professionals within the field would be quick to agree with the following:

1. Grief is normal
2. Grief is not limited to death
3. Grief is not a time-limited event
4. Grief is a unique and individual experience.

However, when you scratch the surface and investigate further, you will see that support programming guidelines remain incongruent with said statements. Despite agreeing that grief is normal, most programs are clinician led and/or supervised. Despite agreeing that grief is not limited to death, most programs only welcome those who have experienced the physical death of an immediate, biological family member. Despite the understanding that grief is not time-limited, most programs only allow clients to join six months after a physical death has occurred and only permit service recipients to remain on service for up to thirteen months before referring them onwards, often to a mental health professional. And finally, despite the agreement and understanding that grief is a unique and individual experience, most programs are geared towards one specific type of griever (intuitive), which we will discuss later in the book. As you can see, the incongruence is quite startling. Despite the sector-wide agreement that grief is normal, the ways in which it orients and engages with both grief and the bereaved are still saturated in Western colonial, pathology-based models of care.

I do not believe that it is enough to say that grief is normal. Normal itself sits in opposition to abnormal. Grief is neither. To grieve is to be *human*. It is one of the very few universal experiences that we as a species share. Regardless of race, ethnicity, class, gender, sexual orientation, or ability, it is a universally guaranteed experience. To live is to grieve. To be human is to grieve. And much to our chagrin, it is an experience that requires neither our consent nor our participation.

The second thing I noticed was the amount of difference that existed in the quality-of-care hospice clients and their families received. For many families, the quality of care received was stunning. In the ten years I spent working in hospices across the province, I saw countless families have truly beautiful end-of-life experiences. I witnessed nurses, volunteers, and care workers go above and beyond the call of duty. I had the great honour of witnessing untold moments of connection and beauty that language would fail to replicate. The families who had these experiences all notably had two things in common: They were white and well resourced. They were families who were well educated and who had both the space and capacity to express gratitude. They were families whose culture and methods of communication mirrored that of the staff and volunteers caring for them. They were families who often went on to become either hospice volunteers, some of hospice's largest donors, or both.

The unspoken underbelly of hospice is that not all families receive equitable quality-of-care. For families that come from under-resourced BIPOC and 2SLGBTQIA+ communities, the experience of end-of-life care is disturbingly different. Families whose culture and methods of communication differ from Western norms are quick to be labelled as difficult. One of the coded ways in which staff will speak to this difference is to designate these families as having "dysfunctional family dynamics" or to snidely attribute their own discomfort to "cultural differences."

I remember coming into work one day and my executive director asked me to lock up the donation box that sat on the reception desk. When I asked why, she told me there was a difficult family in room four and she was afraid the donation box would be stolen. Later that morning, I went in to meet this new family in room four and very quickly assessed that they were not in fact difficult at all; they were poor. She had seen their clothes, heard the way they spoke, and immediately criminalized them for their poverty. The very people that this donation box was meant to serve were being treated as though their mere presence was a threat.

Another noticeable incident was when the hospice I worked at had admitted a South Asian family to its care. They were a lovely, loving, and very large family. The patient had many visitors. There were always plenty of siblings, aunts, uncles, cousins, and community members around him in addition to his immediate family. Throughout their time with us, I noticed a series of weighted comments about the size of the family; how their presence was impeding the nurses from moving about freely in the halls; how the common spaces were all being used by them; and how other (white) families were having to navigate them being there. Comments were made about the smell of the food they brought in and the volume of noise they made when gathering. Previously, when similarly large white families had been in hospice, the dialogue took a noticeably different tone. In these cases, staff would reflect on how much the patient was beloved and how much they had obviously given and meant to their family and community. When food was brought in, staff would praise how generous and thoughtful the family were and would highlight how appreciative they were of the care being provided.

Later when this lovely South Asian man died, his family requested to be in the room while the funeral home prepared the body for removal. Without a moment's hesitation the nurse quickly and sternly said, "That is not allowed." A student I was supervising at the time quickly pushed back and asked, "Why not? I'm happy to speak to the funeral home myself to see what can be done." The nurse stormed away infuriated that she had been questioned publicly by a student. When the student spoke with the funeral home, they were happy to let the family in to witness the preparation of his body. Both family and friends of the deceased resident were aware of the animosity from the staff and expressed gratitude to the student directly for defending their right to be with their loved one's body. The same student was then called into a meeting with the director of residential care and was disciplined for insubordination.

The deep, historic roots of Christianity in hospice care need to be addressed in order to understand these behaviours: "Toward the end of the 19th century, hospices became designated places for the care of terminal patients in Ireland and England. The modern concept of hospice was later developed in England in 1967 by Dr. Cicely Saunders. St. Christopher's hospice was the first hospice under the direction of Dr. Saunders" (Nabili). It is important to note that Dr. Cicely Saunders' vision to establish her own home for the dying was underpinned by her religious faith. She had initially thought of creating an Anglican religious community but broadened her vision so that St Christopher's became a place that welcomed staff and patients of any faith or none. However, as detailed in her profile on St. Christopher's own website, Cicely's strong Christian faith was a fundamental factor in her commitment to the dying and remained an anchor throughout her life. Her philosophy of end-of-life care and the practice of hospice have since spread to many other countries around the world. In the United States and Canada, hospices were originally run by volunteers who cared for dying patients (Nabili). Many of these volunteers were also motivated by, and anchored to, their own Christian faith. It remains the belief of many hospice volunteers today that they are doing both good work and god's work. Because the origins of hospice are so deeply rooted in the Christian faith, it dangerously lacks the anti-oppressive framework of other helping professions, leaving those from equity-deserving communities susceptible to discrimination and harm.

I believe wholeheartedly that grief is universal. That being said, why we experience grief, our access to mourning, and the disproportionate rates in which BIPOC, disabled, chronically ill, and 2SLGBTQIA+ communities experience grief are decidedly not universal. It is not enough to say that grief is normal or universal. To truly support others skillfully, we must be able to name and acknowledge difference. Not in a way that encourages a hierarchy of suffering, or that minimizes anyone's personal experiences of loss, but in a way that says "I see you fully, and I see that your experience of being human is different than my own."

Hospices in Ontario are known for declaring that everyone is welcome. However, saying everyone is welcome is very different than preparing an experience with everyone in mind. If you say everyone is welcome, it implies that all are allowed to attend, but it does not mean they will be able to participate fully when they arrive. Imagine this was a dinner party, and you said everyone is welcome, only to find out you had prepared pasta, and your guests are gluten intolerant. Or perhaps you prepared pork, and you have guests who arrive that are observant Muslims and Jews. Your guests are technically welcome; however, they cannot break bread with you or share in the celebration and connection that food brings. They will not have the experience of being seen, welcomed, or received for who they are. They will simply have been in attendance. In order to create truly inclusive spaces where people can mourn, we must do the work of naming, acknowledging, and preparing for difference.

June 27, 2020

When people ask me about my relationship with Diane, I never quite know what to say. She was older than me and had two young kids. We met over our shared love of music, singing in particular. We were completely smitten with one another. I would spend weeks at a time at her house watching her kids, making meals, singing, listening to music, watching American Idol etc. In order to maximize our time together, she would often pick me up from work, not wanting to lose the time it would have taken me to get to her place on public transit. I remember one time in particular I opened the door to her car, she looked straight at me and said, "I was just driving over here, and I thought to myself who is this angel that has been dropped into my life?" No one, for good reason, had ever called me that before. The love was deep, and then she got sick. Really, really sick. Stage four metastatic melanoma. For reasons I will never fully understand, she invited me to come in close, and together we navigated chemo and clinical trials and treatments. I went to every single appointment with her, and it was the most stunning and most brutal six months of my life. What do you call the kind of love that memorizes and administers dozens of medications daily, the kind of love that sits steadily on the bathroom floor as she screams in pain from the toilet, or the kind of love that goes out searching at all hours of the night for the perfect lemonade slushie because she loves them, and you love her? What do you call the love that makes hundreds of mustard poultices to lay over the tumours protruding from her back and the love that stays in the room and does not look away when the words "there is nothing more we can do" are spoken? What do you call the love that sits vigil for days and weeks on end so there isn't a moment where she is alone, or the love that moisturizes her hands and swabs her mouth and continues to say "I love you. I love you. I love you" long after she can respond? What do you call the love that stays until the final breath is drawn or the love that continues to carry her across continents and lifetimes she will never see? What do you call the kind of love that would do it all over again in a heartbeat regardless of the cost? What do you call such a thing? I don't know. So now when asked, I simply answer what is most true: She was my beloved—the woman whose life and death birthed me forward into my own.

—Rachelle Bensoussan

Chapter One

How Did We Get Here?

An Investigation into the Current Landscape of Grief and Loss

Grief is not a disorder, a disease or a sign of weakness. It is an emotional, physical, and spiritual necessity, the price you pay for love. The only cure for grief is to grieve.

—Earl A. Grollman

This is a quote I have referred to many times throughout my career, and while I agree wholeheartedly with its sentiment, I use it to illustrate how deeply ingrained it is within us to use the language of pathology. Earl A. Grollman is an internationally recognized bereavement counsellor. He deeply believes that grief is not a disorder or a disease, and yet, if you unpack this quote further you will see that his language suggests that grief has a cure. Why would something that is neither disease nor disorder require a cure? What is there to cure one of if there is no disease or disorder present? Our culture is so deeply saturated in pathology-based models of care that even Grollman himself fell prey to its trappings.

In the fifteen years that I have been working with the bereaved, there is one question that they report being asked regularly by well-intended loved ones whenever they begin to outwardly express their grief: are you speaking with someone? The great irony of this question is that in that very moment they are indeed speaking with someone. They are speaking with you. What they really mean to say is "Are you speaking with someone else?" Without fail, the someone else that they are referring to is a professional of some sort, either a physician, social worker, psychologist, therapist and/or mental healthcare provider.

There is an unspoken equation in Western culture that says pain = pathology. Whenever we experience pain or discomfort of any kind, we are quick to reach out to an expert or professional in order to find the solution. There is an equally strong belief that all things can be fixed or healed (i.e., cured). If someone is experiencing long-term chronic pain or distress, whether that be physical or psychological, the belief is that they simply haven't looked or tried hard enough to heal themselves, and the onus is on them to do so. We are taught from a young age that if you have a toothache, you visit a dentist. If your car breaks down, you take it to a mechanic. If your pet is sick, you find a local veterinarian. Whatever the problem is, there is always someone who has the necessary training, skills, and expertise to address it. And it is here, within this faulty equation, where we can begin to source the origin of our culture's pathological orientation to grief.

As of 2024 in Canada, there is not a single graduate level program in medicine, nursing, psychology, social work, or education that requires its students to take a three-credit mandatory course in grief and loss. Not one. Let that sink in for a moment.

There are some programs that offer it as an optional elective; however, the subject of grief is most often tucked into an end-of-life palliative care course rather than a standalone exploration. Remember when I mentioned that most professionals would agree that grief is not exclusive to death? If we all agree that grief is a response to loss, rather than a response to death, then why would it only be covered in an end-of-life palliative care elective? What about all of the people who work in the areas of domestic violence, child welfare, long-term care or addictions? Certainly, they too would benefit from education and training in grief and loss. Even if we were to focus exclusively on death-related grief this still does not explain the placement of grief and loss solely within end-of-life palliative care courses. What about all of the deaths that do not happen from natural causes or illness? What about those who die in accidents, or those who die by suicide, or those who are victims of homicide? The placement of the subject matter alone speaks to the lack of literacy that exists in institutions of higher learning across the country. The professionals who are indisputably on the front lines of grief and loss daily have zero mandated education, training, skills, or expertise in grief and loss. It is entirely absent from their curriculum.

To take this one step further, when doing an overview of nursing curriculum across Canada, the only time grief was mentioned was in reference to Dr. Elizabeth Kübler-Ross's five stages of grief—an idea that was first written about in the 1969 publication of her book *On Death and Dying* and that has long been misrepresented and refuted not only by the bereaved but by Kübler-Ross herself (McVean). Can you imagine the uproar that would arise were we to discover an institute of higher learning that was teaching nursing students clinical skills using methodology and evidence from 1969? For frame of reference in 1969 the American Psychiatric Association had both homosexuality and hysteria listed in the Diagnostic and Statistical Manual as mental health disorders. Yet as of 2024, it is common practice for young nurses to be taught this antiquated, nonevidence-based model of grief.

DID YOU KNOW?

The Myth of Elizabeth Kübler-Ross

- Elisabeth Kübler-Ross published her book *On Death and Dying* in 1969.
- The Kübler-Ross model of grief was not based on empirical or systematic investigations (McVean).
- Kübler-Ross's book is "a collection of case studies in the form of conversations with dying patients" (Parkes 94). She cited her contact with "over two hundred dying patients" (Stroebe et al. 461) as its basis.
- By 2019, despite the lack of evidence to back up Kübler-Ross's model, *On Death and Dying* had still been cited 15,509 times on Google Scholar (McVean).
- Although commonly referenced in popular culture, studies have not empirically demonstrated the existence of these stages, and the model has been considered by some to be outdated (O'Connor) and unhelpful in explaining the grieving process (Bonanno; Stroebe et al.).

- Internationally renowned grief researcher, Kenneth J. Doka, said "Kübler-Ross originally saw these stages as reflecting how people cope with illness and dying, not as reflections of how people grieve."
- Despite having a multitude of evidence-based grief theories to choose from, Kübler-Ross's disproved model of grief remains to this day the most commonly referenced and taught model of grief in North America.

Western culture has taught us to believe that grief is something so fragile and volatile that it can only be engaged with by those with high levels of education and training. We have been taught to believe that non-professionals lack the skills and expertise required to properly support the bereaved and mitigate harm. We treat grief as though it requires the expertise of a cardiovascular surgeon, yet human beings have somehow managed to survive living with loss for nearly two million years, well before the first university was established in 1088. Somehow, millions of humans today continue to live with loss in communities where there are no paid-to-be-there professionals. No therapists. No psychiatrists. Having spent a great deal of time in some of these communities, I will be so bold as to suggest that they are living with loss far more skillfully than a culture that sends their bereaved to professionals who have absolutely no education, training, or expertise in the very subject they are experiencing.

Many of the beautiful humans I have had the deep honor of supporting as they learn to live with loss have found me after painful and pathologizing experiences with varying healthcare professionals. They have been pathologized, misdiagnosed, and treated with a lack of understanding that has only compounded their experiences of grief and loss. When supporting them to unpack these experiences of harm, I will often ask, "Would you take parenting advice from someone who has never parented?" or similarly, "Would you take Spanish lessons from someone who does not speak Spanish?" Author Megan Devine brilliantly writes, "There are some things that cannot be fixed, only carried" (3). As a bereaved person I have come to believe that when learning how to carry something that cannot be fixed, it is most useful to seek out those who have learned to bear the load.

To help folks unpack the assumption that pain equals pathology, I will often ask the following question: What is another experience that we as humans can have that is physically painful, distressing, laborious, and entirely normal? Answer: childbirth. Childbirth serves as a fantastic analogy for grief for many reasons, one of which is the vast degree of variance that can occur in childbirth underneath the umbrella of what we would call normal. This vast degree of variance is similar to that experienced by the bereaved.

On April 26, 2012, I was anxiously awaiting the birth of my baby who was two weeks overdue. I was forty-two weeks pregnant and entirely over the experience as a whole. I had gone for an ultrasound earlier in the day, and my midwife had said that my amniotic fluid was low. I would have to be induced the next morning as it would be against medical advice to allow me to remain pregnant any longer. She decided to admit me to the hospital that night so I could get a good night sleep before the big event. She would return at 6:00 a.m., the following morning to begin the induction. To pass the time, my spouse and I decided to order in food for ourselves, my sister, and my brother-in-law, all who were on hand eagerly awaiting our baby's arrival. To invite Diane's memory into the experience, we ordered in her favorite food: Swiss Chalet rotisserie chicken and French fries. Midway through the meal I instantly began regretting our choice of dinner. My stomach was wobbly, and I kept having to get up to use the washroom. Curiously, every time I got to the washroom, I no longer felt the urge to go. This happened multiple times over the course of the hour until finally, at somewhere around 9:00 p.m., the gentle urge to use the washroom turned into a debilitating pain that could only be recognized as a contraction. I looked at my spouse and said, "I think you should call someone." My spouse looked at my brother-in-law and said, "Can you start timing these?" My contractions had begun, and they continued at less than two minutes apart from that moment forward. By the time a resident could be found, the clock read 9:29 p.m. The resident did a quick check and said, "Yup, you are three centimetres dilated, better call your midwife and have her get back here." At 11:59 p.m. on Thursday, April 26, 2012, after a wild two hours and thirty minutes of labour—that was missed by both my doula and the second midwife—our daughter made her grand entrance. It was a hurricane of a birth to welcome in the most magical of creatures.

My wife, Isabel, had given birth to my stepson, Leo, eight years earlier on a cold, winter night in February of 2004. In complete opposition to my own, her experience of labour was lengthy and increased gradually over time. Her delivery started with twenty-four hours of early labour, followed by eight hours of active labour to get her from four centimetres to full dilation. Once fully dilated, she then pushed for an additional four hours before Leo made his debut.

Both labours occurred without any need for intervention and without any complications. Both of us had natural, nonmedicated, vaginal deliveries. Both labours, though wildly different from one another, were entirely normal. And so herein lies yet another question of interest: Would it be customary for us to attribute personal narratives or characteristics to either of these births? For example, would it be commonplace to say: "Rachelle's uterus displayed great strength and resilience. It truly rose to the challenge beautifully. Her uterus was courageous, capable, and met the circumstances head-on. Her uterus is a true inspiration." To the contrary, would it be fair to say the following about Isabel's uterus? "Hers seemed to be in a significant state of denial. It was obviously stuck and struggled to meet the call of the moment. Overall, her uterus seemed fragile and was unable to rise to the occasion." Of course, I am asking this somewhat tongue-in-cheek—however, I also believe it is a worthwhile line of inquiry. Why is it that these would be absurd things to say about someone's uterus? The reason is because the person in labour had no agency or choice over the kind of labour that ensued. I wasn't given a room service menu in my hospital room the night before where I could choose from a variety of childbirth experiences. It was simply an experience that occurred in the body without my participation or consent. From the moment that first contraction occurred, the train was out of the station. Looking back, I'm not sure I participated much at all, other than to get in the way of what my body was naturally already doing involuntarily. I didn't consent to the labour beginning; I did not consent to it increasing in intensity; and I could not have stopped it from continuing even if I wanted to. And so is true with grief. We are not given a menu of grief responses to choose from. There is no way of saying, "I'll take the insomnia, indigestion, and intrusive thoughts please." There is no way of pre-ordering a serving of lethargy with a side of diminished cognitive capacity. We don't choose how grief shows up. We have zero agency over the matter. It too occurs in the body without our participation and without our consent. Yet how many times have you heard the words "denial," "stuck," or "fragile" used to describe the bereaved? How many times have we judged and created whole narratives about someone's grief experience as though they have a say in what they are experiencing? Saying someone is stuck or in denial, or any other story we may create about another's very own, unique lived experience of grief, is as absurd and inaccurate as it would be to do so in relation to a uterus. Stories are beautiful, powerful things. Some are fiction; some are nonfiction. They can heal, and they can harm. The only person who should ever be telling a story about grief is the person to whom the grief belongs. Period.

How did we get here? How, as a culture, have we arrived at a place where grief, something as natural and human as childbirth, is seen not only as pathology but as something that requires inherent intervention and professionally acquired skills and expertise? When did we lose our collective, innate knowing of what it means to mourn, to live with the inevitable losses that come about as a result of being here, human, and alive? What happened to us, and more curiously, might it have been by design?

When I ask folks to tell me the first word that comes to mind when I say "childbirth," the overwhelming response I receive is "pain." This is because for most of our lives, both implicitly and explicitly, whether through storytelling, personal accounts, and/or depictions shown in media, childbirth is usually portrayed as being both painful and laborious. I remember when I was a young adolescent and would complain about menstrual pain, the resounding response from the older women in my life was "Just you wait..." From my earliest memories, I recall understanding that childbirth, should I choose to experience it, would likely be one of the most physically painful experiences of my life. Because this is what I had always been told and shown, when my contractions began on that spring night in April of 2012, my immediate thought was, "Holy shit! They were right!" I did not panic, and I was not concerned that anything was wrong. I simply knew that what I had been told my entire life was indeed accurate. It was, for me, the single most physically painful experience I had known to date. Now, I want you to imagine something for me. What if our entire lives we had been told both implicitly and explicitly, whether through storytelling, personal accounts and/or depictions shown in media, that childbirth would be a very different experience? What if the story we were told instead went something like this?

One day, should you find yourself pregnant and decide to carry that pregnancy to term, at some point between thirty-eight and forty-two weeks of gestation, your body will suddenly be flooded with a euphoric sensation. You will feel as though you are floating weightlessly through the air. Your body will feel fluid and spacious. It will be an experience of utter ecstasy and bliss. This dreamy experience can last anywhere from four to seventy-two hours at which point you will feel a slight pressure in your lower abdomen, no pain whatsoever, and that will be the indication that your baby is ready to emerge.

If this was the story we were told and shown over and over again throughout our lives, then when a body experienced its first legitimate contraction, the ensuing response would be very different. If the experience you are having is vastly different than the one you were told it would be—and the experience you are having is far more painful, laborious, and distressing than the experience you were told you should be having—there is only one possible thing to think: Something is wrong. It would then make sense to be flooded with panic and to call for immediate assistance. The reason that is not how most people respond when they go into labour is because the experience they are having is congruent to the one they were told they would be having. So, albeit still a highly unpleasant experience, having accurate information as to what you can expect mitigates both the panic and the immediate assumption that something is wrong. This is where we can begin to unpack our culture's current pathology-based relationship with grief.

For most of our lives, both implicitly and explicitly, we in Western culture have been taught one singular and widespread narrative about grief. We have been taught first and foremost that grief is something that occurs only when a member of our immediate, biological family has died. We are taught that grief is a time-limited event, usually lasting anywhere from six to twelve months. We are taught that grief will unfold in a linear, stage like progression where we will experience five predetermined and universal stages: denial, anger, bargaining, depression, and acceptance. We are taught that grief is a temporary disruption to our lives, and should we simply walk ourselves through these five stages, we will emerge on the other side having integrated and adapted to our loss, ready to return to life as normal with no long-standing impact from the loss itself.

This is a fantastic story, one that I wish in many ways were true. However, it is as much a fantasy as the alternative version of childbirth I presented above. These are both stories that are arguably preferable to the actual experiences of birth and grief, but nonetheless they are not representative of the ways that human beings actually experience either. The honest, though far more painful, story about grief, and the one I wish we had the courage to tell instead, goes something like this:

> *Hello, and thank you for being here, human with me. I'm so sorry if you had your heart set on being a reptile or perhaps a bird, but here we are, human. One of the obligatory requirements of human survival is attachment. We can't make it alone; we don't make it alone; we need one another. And one of the great asks of being here, human, is that none of us make it out alive. Not a single one of us. And so, the very thing we need to survive will one day be gone. One day, likely at no fault of your own, the very thing you cannot live without will be no longer. And when this happens, you will be brought to your knees; the pain will be excruciating, likely unlike anything you have ever before experienced. It will feel hard to breath, like your heart is physically breaking. You will look in the mirror and you will not recognize the person staring back at you. Everything you once believed to be true will no longer hold steady. You will be forever changed, and you will learn that there is no normal to return to. The life you once knew, the self you once knew, is gone. And as you look ahead into the terrifying unknown, you will be welcomed into the community of those who are also learning to live without that which they cannot live without. You will find others who are just as lost and disoriented as you are now, and together you will shoulder this great grief. And little by little, day by day, you will somehow learn how to exist, how to survive, well beyond that which you ever thought you could.*

Because the story we have been taught about grief is so deeply inaccurate, it is impossible for us not to think that something is seriously wrong when met with the actual lived experience of grief. It is no different than what our response to childbirth would be had we been taught that childbirth is a highly enjoyable and pleasurable experience. When we are not given accurate information on what it is we will be experiencing, we are then set up to believe that the problem is within us. And in our culture, when there is a problem, we have been socialized to believe that the best way to address it is to seek out professional assistance to fix it. Had we been told the truth about grief from the get-go, we would never assume that something was wrong and would therefore have no need to seek out professional intervention in the first place. When our turn came, and we lost the very thing we could not live without, our only thought would be: "Holy shit! They were right!" We would have no expectations that grief be anything but the laborious and deeply painful experience that it is. We would have no expectation to return to a normal that no longer exists. And we would never for a moment think that anything was wrong with us if we continued to live the rest of our lives right alongside the grief that entered in and changed the very shape of who we were. We would understand it to be as essential to our being as was the attachment from which it was born.

Colonialism has a long record of teaching revisionist histories. In Canada, we have omitted many unpleasant wrongdoings from our history books. We like things tidy and neat; we prefer sanitized versions of the truth. In Canada, we have erased the story of Black slavery, Indigenous residential schooling, and other horrifying atrocities from our curriculum for far too long. We did so to further uphold white supremacy and systemic racial inequities. When certain people's histories and truths are left out of our curriculum, there is clear evidence as to who it benefits and who it harms. Perhaps equally important to note, these truths are not omitted by accident; they are omitted by design.

When I see how grief literacy and education have been completely omitted from our curriculum, it begs the question: who does this benefit, and who does this harm? We know it harms the bereaved to have to live and work in communities, and amongst people, who have no grief literacy. We know that it is harmful to bereaved people to be sent to professionals who have no mandated education or training in grief and loss. We know it is harmful to those who are grieving to be held up to a long-refuted model of grief that in no way reflects their actual lived experience. We also know it is harmful for the nonbereaved to feel as though they are so poorly equipped to skillfully support those they love most in their moments of need. Over and over again throughout my career I've heard from teachers, social workers, counsellors, nurses, and physicians who share with me how much they wish they had had access to grief literacy in their training; how much they want to support their students, clients, and patients with more skill and confidence; and how inept they feel when encountering grief and loss in both their professional and personal lives. So, if grief literacy would only serve to improve the quality of life for both the bereaved and the nonbereaved, why is it being systemically erased from our institutions of higher learning? Who does this benefit?

A mandatory component of all healthcare professionals' curriculum is training in mental health. This is fantastic. Mental health education should absolutely be a core component for anyone who works in these fields. However, when healthcare professionals are taught exclusively about mental health, in the absence of any formal grief literacy or education, something incredibly alarming ensues.

The DSM-5 outlines the following criterion to make a diagnosis of depression. The individual must be experiencing five or more symptoms during the same two-week period and at least one of the symptoms should be either (1) depressed mood or (2) loss of interest or pleasure.

1. Depressed mood most of the day, nearly every day.
2. Markedly diminished interest or pleasure in all, or almost all, activities most of the day, nearly every day.
3. Significant weight loss when not dieting or weight gain or decrease or increase in appetite nearly every day.
4. A slowing down of thought and a reduction of physical movement (observable by others, not merely subjective feelings of restlessness or being slowed down).
5. Fatigue or loss of energy nearly every day.
6. Feelings of worthlessness or excessive or inappropriate guilt nearly every day.
7. Diminished ability to think or concentrate, or indecisiveness, nearly every day.
8. Recurrent thoughts of death, recurrent suicidal ideation without a specific plan, or a suicide attempt or a specific plan for committing suicide.

To receive a diagnosis of depression, these symptoms must cause the individual clinically significant distress or impairment in social, occupational, or other important areas of functioning.

I have spent well over a decade supporting bereaved people who would easily meet every single one of these diagnostic criteria following a significant loss. Who wouldn't be experiencing most of these symptoms after a life-altering, life-shattering loss? If we as a culture tell bereaved people that the only solution to their grief is to seek out professional help and the professionals they meet are exclusively trained in mental health with no mandated education on grief and loss, and the bereaved show up in their offices listing off any and all of the symptoms mentioned above, what do you think will be the inevitable outcome of that encounter? At no fault of their own—these professionals are simply operating from the education and training they did receive—there is no other option but to pathologize the bereaved person in front of them, give them a diagnosis of depression, and treat them accordingly.

In 2019, the global antidepressants market size was 11.67 billion dollars USD ("Antidepressants Market Size"). The market is projected to grow from 14.93 billion dollars USD in 2020 to 18.29 billion dollars USD by 2027. In 2019, national spending on mental health services in the US totalled $225.1 billion and accounted for 5.5 per cent of all health spending. From 2009 to 2019, spending for the US mental health market increased by 52.1 per cent ("The U.S. Mental Health Market"). Given these startling statistics, and the billions of dollars in revenue generated each year, it suddenly becomes quite easy to see why so many stakeholders would have a vested interest in keeping grief and loss education out of postsecondary curriculum. We can start to piece together the larger motivation behind why we, as a culture, have been taught to believe that grief is something best left to the professionals. We can begin to see how and why we have been robbed of our innate knowing and capacity as humans to live with loss. Just as it is in childbirth, we as a species were made to withstand the pain that is required for life to enter into the world; and similarly, we were made to withstand the pain that is inevitable when life exits the world. This does not mean that we have to like it or enjoy it. It simply means that we were built and born with everything already needed inside of us to survive.

I want to explicitly state that I have absolutely nothing but gratitude and awe for pharmaceuticals, and the quality of life they offer to so many. I myself take multiple medications daily to support and manage the chronic conditions I live with. They improve the quality of my life immensely. This is not a critique of pharmaceutical medication itself, but rather a critique of those who seek to profit off the pain of bereaved people by offering clinical and pharmaceutical interventions for a human experience that requires neither.

DID YOU KNOW?

The controversy of prolonged grief disorder (PGD)

- Lisa Cosgrove and Sheldon Krimsky (2012) report that 69 per cent of the DSM-5 task force members reported financial ties to the drug industry, a 21 per cent increase over the prior edition, DSM-IV.
- There is currently a pharmacological randomized controlled study underway conducted by Holly G. Prigerson and her team. This is the same team that lobbied for Prolonged Grief Disorder (PGD) to be adopted in the DSM.
- Prigerson and her team hypothesize that PGD is a disorder of addiction: "The primary gateway symptom for diagnosis is yearning: persistent longing, pining for, or preoccupation with the deceased" (qtd. in Gang). Their description continues, "In this way, patients with PGD continue to 'crave' their loved ones after they have died, due to the positive reinforcement provided by their memories of the loved one" (qtd. in Gang). To break the addiction caused by these memories of the loved one, they are testing a drug used to treat addiction. The drug they are using is called naltrexone.
- The global naltrexone hydrochloride (HCL) market is anticipated to rise at a considerable rate between 2022 and 2030. In 2021, the market was growing at a steady rate and with the rising adoption of strategies by key players, the market is expected to rise over the projected horizon. Due to the COVID-19 pandemic, this market size was estimated to be worth USD 20 million in 2021, and it is forecast to a readjusted size of USD 25 million by 2028 with a compound annual growth rate of 3.3 per cent during the forecast period 2022–2028 ("Naltrexone HCL Market Growth").

IN PRACTICE

Many of my colleagues have publicly denounced the addition of prolonged grief disorder to the DSM. I would like to share with you some of their brilliant insights and critiques here.

Author and psychotherapist, Megan Devine, posted the following on X:

> There's no such thing as prolonged grief disorder. Calling normal human emotion a pathology is a symptom of our "good vibes only" culture. There's NOTHING wrong with you if you're sad, lonely, or have a hard time finding joy or meaning after your person dies. Prolonged grief disorder combines the historical avoidance of pain, plus misogyny, racism & capitalism, PLUS the insurance reimbursement systems that say you can't get help if you aren't "broken," so we need there to be something broken in you that we can fix. If we normalize this very normal human experience, insurance companies won't want to pay for treatment/support, which means a lot of people can't access care if they aren't labeled with a "disorder." And THEN we've got folks who feel they need the official medical diagnosis in order to prove to their friends and family that they have a right to grieve—it's a way to legitimize their feelings and experience, and that's important. This is what I mean friends—addressing the issue of PGD is a whole cauldron of inter-related problems that go far beyond grief itself. It's a symptom of the machinery of capitalism & greed & when you're grieving—you don't always care much about that stuff (with good reason). For now, the short answer of why we've even got a pathology-based view of grief, backed by the medical industry, is capitalism. If you're sad for too long, you're not "productive," and your emotional state is a real downer to the people around you. When you read articles online about prolonged grief disorder and how "the whole world is at risk," remind yourself that grief is normal and healthy, and no one gets to tell you how to grieve. If it helps, read those things, and tell yourself "It's a broken system".

Dr. Donna Schuurman is an internationally recognized authority on grief. In 2022, Donna authored an article entitled, "The Grief Pill is Coming!" Below is an excerpt:

> The drug-related treatment implications of "Prolonged Grief Disorder" are concerning for many reasons, including this ever-growing movement to turn human experiences and challenges into mental conditions. The DSM has a lengthy history of pretending to be scientific, while creating new mental illnesses by consensus among psychiatrists and other mental health professionals as to the existence of these "conditions." Every "mental disorder" in the DSM is a social construct, as Thomas Insel, the Director of the National Institute of Mental Health from 2002–2015 encapsulated in this statement: "While DSM has been described as a 'Bible' for the field, it is, at best, a dictionary ... the weakness is its lack of validity."
>
> Others have not been as kind in their summaries of the DSM. In The Past, Present, and Future of the DSM, Harvard University psychiatrist S. Nassir Ghaemi describes the DSM as "so popular that it became a bible. We've created a bunch of terms—most of which were created out of the blue with no scientific rationale—but just because we would all agree on the definitions. And now we act as if they were handed down by God himself and can never be changed. And that's essentially what's happened in the last 40 years." In the same article, Professor of Psychiatry at the University of Toronto Edward Shorter digs even deeper: "One of the strangely unscientific aspects of the DSM is that it's largely the product of horse trading. People sit down around a big table and say, 'I'll give you your diagnosis if you give me mine.'"
>
> And to add injury to insult, Barry quotes psychiatrist Dr. Paul Appelbaum, the chair of the steering committee overseeing revisions to the DSM's Fifth Edition, whose words insult every parent who has ever had to bury their child as he described people with "Prolonged Grief Disorder": "They were the parents

> who never got over it, and that was how we talked about them… Colloquially, we would say they never got over the loss of that child." When and how did we get to a place where we believe the end goal of grieving the death of a child is to get over it?!
>
> Clearly there is still a lot of work to do for people to become grief-informed and to #UnderstandGrief. As a professional who has worked with children, teens, young adults, parents, and caregivers who are bereaved for over 30 years at Dougy Center: The National Grief Center for Children and Families, who has listened to parents whose children were murdered in school shootings, through wrongful acts of others, in car crashes, and natural disasters, I am disheartened and deeply disturbed by this new diagnosis, and determined to speak on behalf of those who want to be remembered, yearned and pined for after they die. And for those of us who resent being told we have a mental disorder for doing so.

Stefanie Lyn Kaufman Mthimkhulu (they/she), the founding director of Project LETS, wrote an article titled, "Why Prolonged Grief Shouldn't Be Considered a Mental Illness—Especially During a Pandemic." Below is an excerpt:

> In a culture that so often defines mental health by our ability to produce, function, work, minimally impact others, and appear as "normal" as possible, however, there is no space for grief. This makes the addition of prolonged grief disorder to the newly updated DSM, short for the Diagnostic and Statistical Manual of Mental Disorders (aka the "bible of psychiatry"), even more disturbing and misguided. Many of us have been conditioned to believe that a mental illness is just like diabetes—a disease that needs to be managed and treated with medication. But my lived experience, my work in the mental health and disability justice world for over a decade, the wisdom of my community members, and research paints a different picture: Social, political, and economic factors are critical in getting at the root of mental distress and suffering.

> When we think of the myriads of ways marginalized people are denied dignity, humanity, and justice—how long is the "right" amount of time to grieve? Not one loss, but many? Generations? Thousands? Millions? In one way, I imagine it, grief that doesn't go away is a justified response in a world that doesn't allow us to stop, to rest, or be present. Prolonged grief, like madness, is an act of resistance.

As of April 13, 2024, 7,010, 681 people have died of COVID-19 worldwide ("Coronavirus Tracker"). Over seven million humans, from 229 countries and territories, are gone. The vast majority of these deaths occurred between 2020 and 2022. I can't help but question the motivations behind those who in March of 2022 raced to add prolonged grief disorder to the DSM5, following two years of catastrophic loss and a world left bereft in its wake. I can't help but speculate that the millions of people across Canada and the United States who were left in mourning from the pandemic suddenly presented an untapped market ripe for profit.

One of the contributing factors to our overall lack of grief literacy stems from our inadequate understanding of, and the incorrect use of, grief-related language. As a culture, we use the words grief, loss, and mourning interchangeably as though they all mean the same thing. They do not. If we want to lay a strong foundation of grief literacy for ourselves and our communities, we must begin by establishing a shared vocabulary and understanding.

Definitions:

- Grief: our whole being's *involuntary* response to loss
- Loss: the severing from someone or something to whom we have held great attachment
- Mourning: what we *do* with our grief. Mourning describes the activities humans participate in that support the metabolization of grief.

Grief is the involuntary response that humans experience when an attachment is severed. I say involuntary because we do not choose whether it shows up as insomnia or lethargy. We do not choose if we experience deep depression or heightened vigilance. We do not choose if our bodies want to move or collapse. Our culture will tell you that the person who gets up at 5:00 a.m., filled with anxious energy and a mind too busy for sleep, and sets out on a five-mile run, is coping better or healthier than the person who has not left their bed for months. Don't be fooled—this too is simply a story. Both are human. Both are grieving, and neither one had a choice over what their bodies had the capacity or desire to do.

Most of the mechanisms our bodies engage in to keep us alive happen involuntarily. They happen without our participation and without our consent. The very mechanisms that keep us alive and that ensure the survival of our species do not bestow upon us the kind of agency we like to believe they do. A few examples of these mechanisms include breathing, digestion, and reproduction (pregnancy and childbirth in particular). After eating a meal, we don't have to hunker down and spend the next few hours making sure the nutrients go where they are meant to. They don't require our direction or guidance to find their way through our digestive system. We don't need to actively participate in the breakdown of our food or in the separation of nutrients from waste. All of this occurs as we go about our lives. There was never a time when this was clearer to me than when I was pregnant. For forty-two weeks I sat on a couch eating a combination of Toronto street hot dogs and Mike and Ike's. Never once did I have to take out my day calendar and schedule in time to make her gall bladder. I did not have regular Tuesday morning meetings to design her retinas and optic nerves or block off Wednesday evenings to build her reproductive system. For forty-two weeks, without my participation and without my consent, my body went about the business of forming an entirely separate human being—a human being that would soon emerge via yet another mechanism that was equally uninterested in securing my participation or consent. Grief is entirely indifferent to our musings. It does not wait for our permission or acknowledgement to exist.

Our culture often perpetuates the myth that as humans, our deepest, most meaningful attachments are to one another. Despite gross evidence to the contrary, we continue to boast the idea that family comes first, and that in the end, love is all that matters. We need to look no further than North America's response to the COVID-19 pandemic to see how when push comes to shove, our culture very quickly prioritizes the economy over human lives. As humans, particularly those who live within the system of capitalism, we are socialized to have attachments to a myriad of things both tangible and intangible. The list below (Figure 1) is an illustration of just some of the things that we as humans hold deep and meaningful attachments to.

Tangible Losses	**Intangible Losses**
People	Relationships
Homeland	Identity
Job/Employment	Health
Housing	Capacity
Finances	Mobility
Pets	Social status, Capital, Power
Personal Belongings	Hopes & Dreams
	Freedom
	Belonging and Community
	Roles & Responsibilities

Figure 1. Tangible and intangible losses

Grief is an involuntary response to loss. Loss is defined as the severing from someone or something to whom we have held great attachment. This list illustrates the many ways we as human beings may experience both grief and loss outside of death. In fact, death is only one of the numerous ways in which we as human beings experience loss. Our increased literacy depends on our ability to name and recognize grief accurately and to dismantle these antiquated ideas about grief solely being an emotional response to death.

A brilliant mentor of mine once said to me that mourning is our grief gone public—not public as in it requires an audience, but public meaning it is what we do externally with our grief. It is how we take this involuntary and extensive internal experience and bring it outside of ourselves so that it can be digested and metabolized. Rituals of mourning are a tool we can use to metabolize our grief, and they can be either public or private experiences. Rituals of mourning can include lighting candles, participating in memorial events, raising money in memory/honour of someone, creating a scholarship fund in their name, listening to music, dancing, journalling etc. One of the most powerful examples of collective mourning I have seen in recent history was the rise of the Black Lives Matter movement. The movement itself was symbolic of the Black community's grief gone public. The potency of their mourning changed the world. This is the breath-taking power of grief, loss, and mourning.

November 29, 2016

We often believe that grief only manifests itself in feelings. And despite knowing better, I too notice myself defaulting to these misconceptions. So today I noticed myself being surprised by the fact that I felt relatively solid all day, not the usual wobble and internal unease that November brings. I did laundry and watched a movie, enjoyed the time alone while my kiddo was out. I took a shower, and then about half an hour later, I went to dry my hair. As I was doing so, I saw that my hair looked and felt dirty, as though I hadn't in fact washed it at all. As I carried on, it became obvious to me that while I had indeed washed it, I had not rinsed out the conditioner. Why? Who knows. Maybe because even when I'm not deeply emotional, some part of my brain, of me, is still back there with her over a decade ago, wondering what if, remembering the gentle way she introduced me to kale, or thinking of the day she hurled life lessons at the chihuahua from her chair in the living room. Perhaps some part of me is always still back there with her in the car, spontaneously pulling over to get ice cream even though it is winter, being disgusted and amused by how much she loved the French fries and gravy from Swiss Chalet, or feeling the way it felt when she held my hand and invited me to come in close. How baffling it feels to be doing laundry and making dinner and having a relatively trivial day and then remember she's dead. She's still dead. Grief can be thunderous, and it can also be quiet like fresh sheets being draped over the bed. And today, it looks like greasy hair from conditioner that didn't get washed out. I miss you, and I remember.

—Rachelle Bensoussan

Chapter Two

Grief Is NOT a Feeling

Although our culture espouses many myths and misconceptions about grief, there is one particular misconception that I believe is the root cause of considerable harm. Our culture, and the professionals who operate within it, often orient and relate to grief as though it is a feeling. I cannot emphasize strongly enough that grief is not a feeling. Grief is not a feeling any more than we would say childbirth is a feeling. This is not to say that we don't have a multitude of feelings while birthing and grieving; it is to say that the experience as a whole is so much bigger and all-encompassing than a single emotion. Feelings, by nature, are transient. They come and they go, similar to the weather. While birthing, what we feel can change significantly depending on whether we are at the peak of a contraction or resting in between them. While grieving, we can experience hundreds of different emotions in the span of a single hour. Despite the myriad of feelings we may have in both childbirth and in grief, to say that they are strictly emotional experiences would be both inaccurate and reductionist. They are experiences that change who we are permanently; they change our bodies, minds and hearts forever. Human beings are not just our emotions. We also have physical bodies, cognitive thoughts and abilities, social connections and attachments, sexual identities and desires, spiritual or secular beliefs and worldviews. As humans we are a complex, layered, and intricate mosaic of all these collective parts.

Both childbirth and grief are human experiences that impact us on every level of our being and personhood. We would never suggest to someone who was in the throes of childbirth to simply explore and express their feelings as an antidote to their physical pain. We would never encourage someone who was in active labour to sit down with a therapist and explore what exactly they are finding challenging as a strategy to move the labour along. Using a midwifery model of care, we understand that a person who is birthing is occupied; they are busy attending to something that requires all of their focus, energy, and attention. We do not ask those who are birthing to schedule carpool, meal prep, attend work meetings, or engage in meaningful conversations. We understand that they are not in control of what is happening to them and that it will take as long as it takes to get to the other side. We don't question the validity of their pain or doubt how difficult they are finding it. The beautiful thing within this model is that while we wholeheartedly trust and believe in the birthing person's capacity, we don't leave them alone. We stay. We bear witness to their pain and act as support staff should they have a need or request to help them cope with and manage the pain (ice chips, a massage, a heating pad, etc.). We don't assume that we know best or that we know what will feel comforting or supportive to them; we ask. We know that their pain is not optional, yet we trust that they have everything they need within them to make it through. We also know that once the labour is complete, the real work of parenting begins. The labour may be an end to the pregnancy, but it is only the beginning of what is to become a lifetime journey of parenting. Even if the birthing person does not have a live birth, or if at some point across their lifespan their child dies, they remain a parent for the rest of their lives. They will never go back to the person they were before. There are experiences we endure as humans that leave their mark permanently and indelibly on our bodies, minds and hearts. Birth and grief are two of these experiences.

To further investigate the notion that grief is not a feeling, I would like to offer an overview of recent research exploring the holistic impacts of grief. This is by no means a comprehensive, deep dive into the research but rather a synopsis to illuminate the myriad of ways grief can impact us, including and beyond the emotional sphere.

The Physical Impact of Grief

A range of studies have confirmed the vast effects grief can have on the human body. Grief increases inflammation (Fagundes et al.). It damages the immune system, leaving the body depleted and vulnerable to infection (O'Connor). A recent study found that among the elderly, in particular, the recent loss of a loved one may leave a person more vulnerable to infectious diseases due to reduced function in their neutrophils—a white blood cell used to fight off infections (Vitlic et al.). Grief can increase blood pressure and heighten the risk of blood clots (Buckley et al.). Grief has been found to exacerbate physical pain (Bradbeer et al.), and in another study, the flu vaccine was proven to be less effective in older people who had lost a loved one within the past year (Phillips et al.). A great deal of research focuses on the ways that grief can affect the heart muscle along with cardiovascular functioning. Intense grief can alter the heart muscle so much so that it causes takotsubo cardiomyopathy, also known as broken heart syndrome, a form of heart disease with the same symptoms as a heart attack (LeWine). A 2012 study found that a person's risk of having a heart attack increased twenty-one times over in the day immediately following the death of a loved one and six times over the following week (Mostofsky et al.). Other research found that the risk of heart attack or stroke after losing a partner stayed elevated for as long as a month (Carey et al.). Research has shown that grief frequently leads to changes in the endocrine, immune, autonomic nervous, and cardiovascular systems (Osterweis et al.). Sourced from a variety of institutions, including the University of California, Berkeley, WebMD created the following graphic (Figure 2, next page) to illustrate some of the most common ways that grief can affect the human body.

I share a snapshot of this research to show the harm that can occur when grief is viewed strictly through an emotional lens. If we view grief solely as an emotion, we may miss signs and symptoms that require medical attention and care. It also demonstrates why the suggestion that bereaved people should simply feel their feelings is an insufficient approach to skillful grief support. Feeling one's feelings is fantastic, and I encourage one to do so should they find it beneficial, but it is not a be-all and end-all solution for decreased immune function, inflammation or sleep and appetite disturbances. The physical impacts of grief on the human body are real and scientifically verifiable. Those who are grieving need to be believed and offered the same care and compassion as those who are living with other forms of illness. We would also do well to include this research on the physical impacts of grief in medical and nursing curriculum so health care providers can be trained on taking loss histories from their patients in addition to their medical histories.

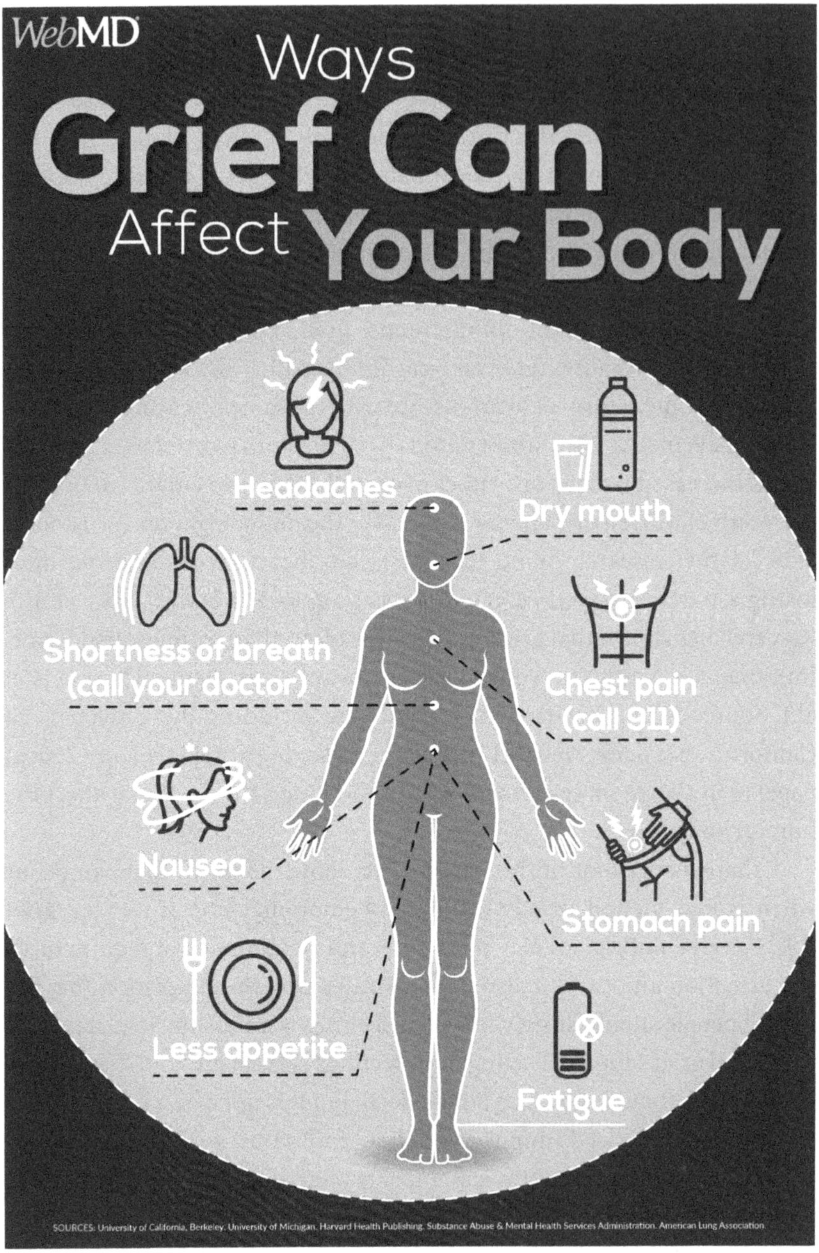

Figure 2. WebMD, "Ways Grief Can Affect Your Body" (Hairston)

The Cognitive Impact of Grief

Grief brain and *grief fog* are common terms often used by the bereaved to explain their experience of cognitive impairment following a loss. They can include, but are not limited to, the following:

- Difficulty completing tasks
- Altered perception of time
- Forgetfulness and confusion
- Impaired attention and memory
- Trouble thinking clearly
- Challenges with decision making
- Difficulty processing information
- Executive functioning impairment

When we experience grief, our brain can perceive it as a threat to our survival. Our brains can go into fight, flight, or freeze mode. This can impact one's brain in a way that worsens memory, cognition, and concentration. You might feel spacey, forgetful, or unable to make well-thought-out decisions. It might also be difficult to speak or express yourself. Things like planning, problem solving, and decision making become unusually challenging. Five studies in particular discuss the neurological impacts of grief due to the death of a loved one. All five studies report activation in the following areas of the brain: the anterior cingulate cortex (ACC), posterior cingulate cortex (PCC), prefrontal cortex (PFC), insula, and the amygdala (Silva et al.). Mounting evidence suggests that grief adversely affects neurological (Freed et al.) and attentional (Schneck, Tu, Michel, et al.) processes and is associated with lower performance in decision-making tasks (Fernández-Alcántara et al.).

Many of the challenges listed above are similar to the challenges people face when living with disabilities that impact executive functioning. The above list could also be used to describe some of the cognitive impacts of those who live with acquired brain injuries. When we think of those who live with disabilities that impact cognitive and executive functioning, or those who live with brain injuries, it is not hard to understand how the impacts of grief can also be disabling. I often think of how our culture and medical system treat people who have acquired a brain injury, perhaps through a motor vehicle accident or some other sudden event. Once the person is stabilized, we don't discharge that person from the hospital and expect them to resume the full responsibilities of their life prior to the accident. Ideally, once someone is stabilized, we send them to rehab where something amazing happens. They are welcomed by an interdisciplinary team of professionals with actual skills, expertise, and training in brain injuries. They are surrounded by other people who are also learning how to adapt to their new reality including some very real limitations. Those who are there to support them don't placate them with false hope and euphemisms but rather get to know them as the unique individuals they are in order to cocreate a care plan reflective of what is most important to them. Together, they map out small, attainable goals that reflect the reality of their circumstances. No one pretends they will return to who they once were. No one denies that something significant and life altering has occurred. Everyone the person is surrounded and supported by acknowledges that this event has, and will, permanently change both their reality and their capacity. It is also understood that it will take an entire community to support this person's adaptation and integration into this new normal.

Can you imagine if we applied a similar model of care to the bereaved? What if after a significant loss, a bereaved person could receive care from a community of people who have skills, expertise, and training in grief and loss? What if they could choose to go somewhere where they were surrounded by other bereaved people? What if they could go to a place where there was a fundamental understanding that they have been changed permanently and that they will never again return to the person they once were; a place where they did not have to resume the full responsibilities of their lives after only three days; a place that openly acknowledges the true amount of time and support it will require for them to metabolize and adapt to what has occurred? Were we to truly acknowledge the depths to which the bereaved are impacted cognitively by grief, we would never see fit to ask them to resume the full responsibilities of their lives after a three-day bereavement leave. We would infer how truly irresponsible this would be to both the bereaved person and to those in their orbit, both professionally and personally. Were we to truly grasp how cognitively disabling the experience of grief can be, we would likely have so much more compassion and space for the ways that bereaved people are able to show up and for the efforts they are making to adapt. Instead of judging them for a messy home or missed appointment, we could shift our gaze to the amazing things they are doing. We could celebrate and praise them for brushing their teeth or taking a shower. We could acknowledge the actual labour and energy it takes to get the kids to school or make a meal. Similar to those who have survived a life-threatening event, what if instead we simply sat back and marvelled at the gift of their survival regardless of how long and bumpy the road ahead may be?

The Emotional Impact of Grief

While grief itself is not a feeling, we do experience countless, varying feelings while we are grieving. Another misconception we hold is that grief is experienced predominantly as sadness or sorrow. While our culture is highly grief illiterate, we are also quite emotionally illiterate. When asked to describe what grief feels like most people will say sad or mad. This demonstrates, at best, a preschool level of awareness as to the ways grief can impact us emotionally. Take a look at the feelings word cloud below (Figure 3) to sample just some of what one might experience while they are grieving:

Figure 3. "Emotions Word Cloud Collage, Social Concept Background"

Often times, when working with bereaved folks, it can be useful to support them in growing their emotional vocabulary. If someone says they are sad, it can be useful to ask, "When you say you are sad, are you yearning? Are you longing? Do you feel despondent or perhaps inconsolable?" These are all different feelings. If someone says they are angry, it can be useful to ask, "Are you furious? Are you irritable? Are you impatient?" Again, these are all different. Supporting the bereaved to be specific in what they are experiencing can help them to identify the unmet need underneath the feeling. If someone is longing, what are they longing for? For example, if someone has experienced the death of a partner, perhaps in addition to longing for the return of their partner, one can explore which particular parts of their partner's presence it is they are longing for. Perhaps they share that they long for physical touch or to be held. Although we can't meet their ultimate need of bringing their partner back, perhaps it is worthwhile exploring who they have in their life they could ask to be held by (a sibling, friend, parent, etc.). Often times when we are so overwhelmed by loss, we can unintentionally throw the baby out with the bathwater and create a reality where none of our needs can be met, compounding our experiences of grief and loss. When we increase our own emotional vocabulary and get specific about what it is we are feeling, it can offer us the opportunity to explore what the unmet need is underneath the feeling itself. It is here where we can uncover other possibilities and opportunities for getting that need met, even if it cannot come in the form in which we are originally used to receiving it. It is not true that all needs can be met, and they certainly cannot be met all the time; however, given that not all things can be fixed or restored, it is useful to be cognizant of where we do have opportunities to receive care and comfort in order to not add additional, unnecessary loss to an already considerable load.

Alfred A. Montapert once said, "Do not confuse motion and progress. A rocking horse keeps moving but does not make any progress." Given that grief can often feel painful and heavy for months and years on end, supporting the bereaved in recognizing that movement is indeed taking place, even when it feels unpleasant, can be a crucial component to them recognizing their own progress. When a bereaved person can identify that six months prior they were feeling predominantly enraged and now their most prevalent feeling is one of irritability, that *is* progress even when both feelings are undesirable. It can feel both hopeless and insurmountable in the early years of grief if we experience it as one, singular, abiding experience of pain. To be experiencing the same thing for months and years on end is demoralizing and impairs our ability to imagine a future that might look or feel any different than our current reality. If we can support the bereaved and ourselves in noticing and naming the ever-changing, transient nature of our feelings—however unpleasant they may be—we can breathe a little easier recognizing that we are in fact in motion and indeed making progress towards whatever it is that comes next.

I want to specify that while many people experience grief as painful and distressing, this too is not the only way that grief impacts us emotionally. Many people experience relief, emancipation, and even joy as part of their journey through grief. Another common misconception about grief is that we only grieve things we have loved, cared for, or held in positive regard. Nothing could be further from the truth. As we learned previously, the only thing required for grief to be present is attachment—not love or fondness but attachment. Many of us have held deep attachment to those who have harmed us. Many of us have held great attachment to people, relationships and experiences we've never met or known. It is also not uncommon for people to feel considerable relief and spaciousness after losing something or someone that has taken up a great deal of their life's energy and attention (e.g., an abusive partner, caregiving for elderly parents, or long-time cycles of addiction). Just as we do not choose how grief shows up in our physical bodies, we also do not choose the feelings that arise while we are grieving. Given that all feelings are valid, we would do well to welcome them in when they arrive and, similarly, allow them to move along when ready as opposed to inviting them in for a more permanent stay.

Three months after Diane died, I went to a bereavement support group for those who had experienced the death of a loved one to cancer. I was twenty-five at the time and was the youngest member of the group by at least twenty years. The person closest in age to me was a woman in her forties whose husband had died, leaving her the single parent of three young children. She was a very quiet, introverted person and did not often share much in the group. During one of our sessions, the experience of guilt kept arising among the participants. Many people reflected on times in the previous week when they had caught themselves smiling or laughing and then immediately were flooded with feelings of guilt for having a good time given the circumstances. In a moment I will remember for the rest of my life, the quiet, introverted woman spoke up using her full voice and said, "I refuse to feel guilty for a brief moment of reprieve when hell has already arrived." It is a sentence I will never forget. In a single moment, she so beautifully articulated the fleeting and transient nature of the emotions that live and breathe right alongside the permanency of grief.

IN PRACTICE

Increasing your emotional literacy.

One of the things I love to suggest to folks who are interested in increasing their emotional vocabulary is the following exercise. Use the internet to search for a comprehensive feelings list. There are plenty of them available to download as a PDF, free of charge. Print out this list and keep it next to your bed. At a time of day that best suits you (right when you wake up or before you go to bed), set aside five minutes uninterrupted to check in with yourself. I recommend closing your eyes and taking a few deep breaths to ground yourself. As you do so, scan yourself for what it is you are feeling. Remember to take stock of what you are actually feeling, not what you think you are feeling. When you are ready, open your eyes, and read through the list of feelings you've printed off, highlighting or circling any of those that resonate with you in that moment. Do this once a day for thirty days. At the end of thirty days, you will have hundreds of new feelings words in your vocabulary. You may also discover you have developed a deeper understanding of the transient and fleeting nature of our emotions, in addition to noting the vast range of feelings one can experience in a simple twenty-four-hour period. I find this exercise reminds me that while I want to deeply honour my feelings as valid, I don't want to rely on them as the sole source of information when making important decisions given that they seem to change as quickly as the weather does here on a spring day in Toronto.

The Existential Impact of Grief

The term "assumptive world" was proposed by Murray Parkes, who defines it as "a strongly held set of assumptions about the world and the self which is confidently maintained and used as a means of recognizing, planning and acting" (132). The assumptive world theory refers to the assumptions or beliefs that ground, secure, stabilize, and orient people to the world around them. Ultimately, they are the core beliefs that shape how we experience the world we inhabit. In the face of death or trauma, these beliefs are shattered, and complete disorientation enters the lives of those most impacted. In essence, the security and certainty of their beliefs have been confronted, challenged and shattered.

The theory of shattered assumptions was developed and detailed by psychologist Ronnie Janoff-Bulman in her 1992 book *Shattered Assumptions: Towards a New Psychology of Trauma*. According to Janoff-Bulman, most people hold three fundamental assumptions about the world that are constructed and substantiated over years of lived experience:

1. **The world is benevolent.** This assumption speaks to our overall belief in the goodness or virtue of the world. This assumption alludes to the benevolence of the world as an entity and the benevolence of the people who inhabit that world.

2. **The world is meaningful.** This assumption addresses why certain events happen in our world, in addition to why they happen to certain people. A meaningful world is one that makes sense. It is one in which we see the connection between a person's behaviour and character and how they experience the world. We assume that a good person will experience good things and that people who behave correctly can avoid negative outcomes, such as serious illness or tragedy. Consequently, we expect bad people to experience bad things. With these assumptions, we create an assumptive world that makes sense; such a world is predictable and assures us that what happens to us is not random.

3. **I am worthy.** This assumption positions oneself as a positive, moral, and decent person and therefore as one who is deserving of the world's benevolence. This assumption enables us to maintain a belief that we can control the events that will occur across our lifespans.

These unspoken assumptions provide humans with a sense of safety, wellbeing, and relative invulnerability that enables us to awake each morning and face the day (Mills). Shattered assumptions theory proposes that experiencing death or traumatic events can change how humans view themselves and the world. Specifically, the theory explores the effects that death or trauma can have on the three core assumptions listed above. According to Janoff-Bulman, death and traumatic life events shatter these core assumptions, and coping involves rebuilding a viable assumptive world.

I remember clearly the night Diane died. I remember seeing her body and being immediately confronted and disturbed by its stillness. At the time of her death, she had already been unresponsive for days, and as such, I was intimately familiar with the rise and fall of her chest, the sound of her exhale. I was deeply attuned to the smallest grimace or shift in her respirations. When she finally died, the complete stillness and silence of her body were impossible for me to process. Seemingly out of nowhere, a thought popped into my head. *This must be a mistake. It wasn't her time to go.* What did I mean by that, and where had this thought come from? I knew she was dying. I had been anticipating her death for weeks, and in the past forty-eight hours, it had become apparent that her death was imminent. So why would I think that it was a mistake? If you had asked me in the months before her diagnosis if I believed that people only die when it is their time, I don't know that I would have been able to identify that as a belief for myself; however, in the moment of being confronted with my beloved's still, dead body, that unconscious assumption emerged and was shattered. Some part of me must have held an unconscious belief that when people die, it is because it was their time to go. Yet in seeing her life complete with so much of it left unfinished, my assumption was revealed, and its validity exposed.

Rebuilding one's assumptive world—or learning to live in a world where one's assumptions have been shattered—is the lifelong task of every bereaved person. How does someone decide to risk falling in love again after their beloved has died? How does someone decide if they want to get pregnant again after their baby is born still? How do you carry on in a world that you now know to be unpredictable, random, and unjust? These are not questions that have easy answers; nor are they questions that any two bereaved people will answer the same way. Reorienting oneself without the safety net of an assumptive world is a painful, arduous, and deeply personal expedition—one that will take the entirety of one's lifetime to complete. When bereaved people say they will never get over their loss, move on, or go back to who they once were, this is what they are referring to. You don't ever get to go back to the person whose assumptive world remains intact once yours has been shattered.

The Social Impact of Grief

Human beings are social creatures. Social creatures are those who remain highly interactive with members of the same species and whose psychological well-being is associated with social interactions (Animal Care and Use Office). Examples of nonhuman social creatures would include but are not limited to canines, primates, elephants, dolphins, and whales. As social creatures, we are biologically designed to need this connection with others as much as we need oxygen, food, and water. This is informed by several decades of research in the fields of attachment theory, social baseline theory, and neuroscience. Given this essential need for attachment, it is easy to understand how our social worlds are often as deeply impacted by loss as we are. The term "secondary losses" is often used to refer to the losses a bereaved person experiences in their social world as the result of a primary loss. Secondary losses can include but are not limited to the loss of relationships, finances, future plans, etc.

Bereaved people tend to experience the deterioration of long-standing relationships both within and outside their family systems. Over and over again, I have heard hundreds of bereaved people share with me the deep loss and disappointment they experience when the people they love most fail to show up for them in meaningful ways. I have not yet met a single bereaved person who has not experienced the loss of at least one close relationship as a result of being bereaved. Alternatively, the majority of bereaved people also report being pleasantly surprised by the people who do show up in meaningful ways, particularly those who may not have been on their radars previously as the ones most likely to do so.

Bereaved people experience both implicit and explicit avoidance by peers, colleagues, and friends. Every bereaved person has the experience of bumping into someone at work, or perhaps at the grocery store, and immediately seeing the discomfort wash over the other person's face. This is usually followed by some clumsy interaction where the nonbereaved person spits out some platitudes about how everything happens for a reason or how the universe doesn't give you more than you can handle while they attempt to end the conversation and scurry away as quickly as humanely possible. The bereaved person's mere presence casts a spotlight onto the fragility of the others' assumptive world.

Intimate loneliness, or what sociologist Robert Weiss terms "emotional loneliness," refers to the perceived absence of a significant someone (e.g., a partner, friend, confidant)—that is, a person one can rely on for emotional support during crises and who provides mutual assistance and affirms one's value as a person. This corresponds to what biological anthropologist and evolutionary psychologist Robin Ian MacDonald Dunbar describes as the "inner core," which can include up to five people (the "support clique") and comprises the people we rely on for emotional support during crises. Often when a bereaved person experiences a loss that is not shared or understood by their support clique, the experience of intimate loneliness can emerge. This is especially true when someone loses the person they perceive to be their significant other or the one with whom they relied on previously in times of crisis and distress.

After experiencing secondary losses, intimate loneliness, and the implicit and explicit avoidance of others, it is no wonder why bereaved people often change their behaviour to comply with socially sanctioned expressions of grief. To avoid experiencing any of the above, bereaved people learn quickly how to shapeshift in order to present a sanitized version of their reality to the world. Despite not being an authentic representation of their lived experience, bereaved people may find themselves saying things like "I am grateful they are no longer suffering" or "At least I know I am able to get pregnant" in an attempt to minimize the significance of their loss and make their reality more palatable to others.

Finally, bereaved people often experience a pronounced shift in their priorities following a loss. A book club that once served as a place for community and the exchange of ideas can suddenly feel futile and isolating. The camping trip you used to look forward to every summer can quickly feel overwhelming and unmanageable. Your career ambitions, goals that for years felt solid and clear, can change overnight and suddenly your dreams feel trite and trivial. There is no way to predict all the ways that grief will come in and change who you once were. It is never just the initial loss itself that a bereaved person has to metabolize. It is all of these secondary losses that follow, including, and perhaps most importantly, the loss of oneself.

The Sexual Impact of Grief

Grief is a complex topic. We've already established that we do not openly talk about grief in our culture, nor do we portray it accurately. Sex is another complex topic, one that we also do not talk about openly or portray accurately. It should then come as no surprise that there is little public discourse on the ways that grief can impact us sexually. Sex therapist Laurie Watson and couples therapist George Faller are the cohosts of a podcast called Foreplay Radio—Couples and Sex Therapy. During a recent episode, they explored grief through the lens of sexual intimacy. They shared that it is not uncommon for people to respond to grief by either losing all feelings of sexual desire or experiencing heightened sexual needs (20:34–21:40). I have heard the stories of bereaved people who have landed on both ends of this continuum. Some will say, "I am so saturated in grief right now I can't even imagine having sex. My body feels so raw and exposed that the very thought of intimate touch feels repulsive and agitating to me." Alternatively, I have heard others say, "Sex makes me feel fully embodied and alive. It not only offers me relief from this grief, but it also allows me to experience the beauty and joy of being in a body, of being human, of being alive, and I want as much of that as I can have right now." Often when bereaved people have been up close and personal to death and dying, their experience of the world changes and things that might have at one time been forbidden or taboo suddenly become permissible and desirable. It is also not uncommon for people who are grieving to alternate between both ends of this continuum depending on a multitude of factors.

One of my favourite essays ever written about how grief can impact us sexually is an essay written by Cheryl Strayed titled, "The Love of My Life." I strongly encourage you to read it. Below is a small excerpt from it:

> We aren't supposed to want our mothers that way, with the pining intensity of sexual love, but I did, and if I couldn't have her, I couldn't have anything. Most of all I couldn't have pleasure, not even for a moment. I was bereft, in agony, destroyed over her death. To experience sexual joy, it seemed, would have been to negate that

reality. And more, it would have been to betray my mother, to be disloyal to the person she had been to me: my hero.

In this chapter, we have explored some of the ways that grief can impact us physically, cognitively, emotionally, existentially, socially, and sexually. I encourage you to remember that this was just an overview of the latest research, the tip of the iceberg if you will. I hope that after reading this chapter, you will appreciate how reductionist it is, and therefore how harmful it can be when we relate to grief solely as an emotion. While feelings are temporary and passing, the impacts of grief are lifelong. If we want to be able to support ourselves and others skillfully—with generosity, grace, and compassion—we would be best served to remember that grief, like parenting, is an experience that only concludes when we do.

November 29, 2017

I had a moment today where I was once again confronted with how much grief is a primary aspect of my being. How much it informs the way I live my life and the choices I make. How much a part of self it has become. How inseparable I am from it.

My love is coming home tomorrow after what feels like a very long absence. So, today I spent much of the afternoon cleaning and washing bedding and making sure there were fresh cut flowers by the window—all the things that say, welcome home, rest, I missed you.

I don't wash the bedding while she is away because it helps sometimes to fall asleep with the smell of her on the sheets. But then this afternoon, as I went to strip the bed (so she would have clean, fresh sheets to slip into tomorrow), I froze and was flooded with fear and caution. What if she doesn't make it home? It's still twenty-four hours away and so much can happen, and then I would have washed away the smell of her on the sheets. I looked around not knowing what to do and saw her t-shirts hanging from the door. They too smelled like her, so I took the risk and washed the bedding.

As the bedding was in the laundry, I found my way into the hall closet searching for the blue blanket I keep tucked away in a box that was once saturated with the smell of another love. I remember the day I took it out and could no longer smell her on it because it had been many so many years since.

It is November, again, and this year it will be twelve years since I last heard her voice or felt her hand in mine. And despite no longer being able to recall the names of her medications, or the precise smell of her skin, I continue to live each day with the dull ache of longing.

—Rachelle Bensoussan

Chapter Three

When Did Being Human Become So Wrong?

As we explored in Chapter Two, grief is not a feeling. To say so is to reduce one of the most intense and transformational human experiences into a singular emotion. The often-unintended result is a complete lack of understanding and appreciation for the biological imperative of grief. This misconception causes us to perceive grief as something unpleasant that must be addressed or resolved, as something that requires interference or intervention instead of a natural, life-affirming, species-sustaining mechanism employed involuntarily by the body. But how can something so seemingly disruptive and exhausting be life-sustaining, you might ask? The answer has been hiding in plain sight.

If we look closely at some of the life-sustaining mechanisms the human body employs to keep itself, and our species, alive most of them have the following elements in common:

- Each of these mechanisms occurs involuntarily
- Each of these mechanisms are cyclical or recurring, meaning they cannot occur once and be considered complete or sufficient.

Let's look closely at a few examples. We can start with what is arguably the most important of these mechanisms: breathing. Without oxygen, a human being cannot survive beyond four to six minutes. Breathing is one of the ways medical professionals determine whether someone is alive or dead. Breathing is something that we all do involuntarily, and it is something that we must continue to do regularly for the rest of our lives to remain alive. We cannot complete a single inhale/exhale cycle and consider ourselves set, and unless someone were to stop breathing, we don't ever interfere or intervene with one's natural respirations. We understand it to be a necessary and vital function of life.

Another requirement for sustaining life is hydration and nutrition. Similar to breathing, these are not needs that can be satiated once and considered complete. For humans to survive, they must be engaged in the recurring cycle of ingestion, digestion, metabolization and elimination. The process of digestion is, again, an involuntary one. Once we've consumed food or water, we don't have to allocate time in our day to make sure the nutrients and vitamins find their way to their rightful place in the body. We don't have to schedule time in our agendas to make sure the waste finds its way into, and through, the small intestines. Every minute of every day, almost entirely on their own accord, our bodies are somewhere in the digestive cycle. We don't become guides and orchestrators of the process. We simply go about our lives while our bodies do the heavy lifting, requiring neither our participation nor consent.

For humans to survive as a species, reproduction is required. Pregnancy and childbirth are the two final mechanisms I would like to explore. When a body is pregnant, there is nothing that the pregnant person has to do to actively participate in the development of the fetus. Pregnant people do not get time off of work to design and create the fetus's endocrine system. Pregnant people do not spend their weekends meticulously working on their fetus's fingers and toes. I can report from personal experience that when I was pregnant, I spent the majority of my forty-two-week pregnancy complaining, and still, forty-two weeks later, a fully formed and functioning human emerged from my body. The human that emerged was formed and developed with little, if any, participation from me. Once again, I sat back, and let my body do the heavy lifting. My experience of childbirth was no different. At a time of its choosing, and little concerned with whether I had consented, my body determined all on its own when it was time for the fetus to make its exit. Again, with absolutely no valuable participation from me, my body knew exactly what to do. It contracted involuntarily, dilated involuntarily, broke my waters involuntarily, and even began to push when it was ready to do so. I can assure you that any intervention or interference that occurred was solely employed to support my ineptitude as I was begrudgingly dragged along the single most wild ride of my life.

I am not saying, nor would I ever imply, that we as a species never require intervention or interference, support, or accommodations when it comes to breathing, digestion, pregnancy, or childbirth. Such a statement is not true. We are not all in the same bodies, and we are not all having the same experiences. I share these analogies to illustrate and illuminate how often we assume, and like to believe, that we have full agency and control over every aspect of our lives when that is simply not the case. The vast majority of what keeps us alive as a species does not exist because we are morally superior or because we have willed it into being. We simply happen to be one of the very lucky few who, despite the odds, have found ourselves here, human and alive.

When we look at each of these cyclical or recurring mechanisms, another thing they all have in common is an element of elimination. The process of elimination helps to make room for more of whatever it is the body requires next (i.e. oxygen, nutrients, offspring). Breathing requires an exhale of carbon dioxide to make room for the following inhale of oxygen; digestion requires that you poop to make room for additional nutrients; and reproduction requires that the fetus exits the uterus to make room for future offspring. However unpleasant or painful things like pooping or childbirth may be, they are a biological necessity for our species to survive. We are not required to like it, but it is a nonnegotiable part of being human. And so is grief.

Grief is our bodies' involuntary response to a severed attachment. Like breathing, hydration, nutrition, and reproduction, attachment is another involuntary mechanism required for human survival. And herein lies the great ask and the great bind of being here human. We need each other to survive, yet not one of us will make it out alive. Oomph. Let that land for a minute. We cannot survive without attaching, yet 100 per cent of us will die. With a bind like that, it would serve to reason that we would have gone extinct as a species quite some time ago. It doesn't feel like a great set up for success or survival. Yet here we are, and here we remain. But how, you might ask? If we require attachment to live, and attachments are constantly being severed and lost, is there some kind of biological mechanism in place to account for these inevitable losses? There is, and it has a name: grief.

DID YOU KNOW?

Attachment Theory

Attachment theory is a psychological, evolutionary, and ethological theory concerning relationships between humans. The most important tenet is that young children need to develop a relationship with at least one primary caregiver for normal social and emotional development. Within attachment theory, "attachment" means an affectional bond or tie between an individual and an attachment figure (usually a caregiver). Attachment theory is not an exhaustive description of human relationships, and it is not synonymous with love and affection, although these may indicate that bonds exist. The theory proposes that children attach to carers instinctively for survival and, ultimately, genetic replication. The biological aim is survival, and the psychological aim is security (Hicks and Korbel).

Grief is the evolutionary solution to the inevitable severing of attachments humans will experience across their life spans. Grief is our body's natural, built-in mechanism for digesting and metabolizing loss in order to make room for new life-sustaining attachments. Similar to how pooping makes room for more food, childbirth makes room for more offspring, and exhaling makes room for more oxygen, grief is what makes room in the body for additional attachments. Although we may like a design makeover for grief, poop, and childbirth, we cannot deny their biological functions or how they sustain us as a species. When we begin to understand how life-sustaining and functional grief is, we can begin to challenge the idea that grief is something that should be fixed, resolved, or interfered with in any capacity. Why would we ever want to be rid of something so essential to our wellbeing? However unpleasant, we would never want to stop pooping. In fact, constipation can lead to increased pain and discomfort, and if left untreated can have serious implications on one's health. However painful childbirth may be, we would never want to remain pregnant forever. The body can only sustain so much before the pain of childbirth is seen as a welcome relief from the lengthy, exhausting experience of pregnancy. Similarly, regardless of how arduous and depleting grief can be, if we can relate to it as something that is ultimately moving us towards more attachment, and therefore more life, we can begin to see grief from an entirely different point of view, one that is ideally much more welcoming and understanding. We can begin to explore how we might best metabolize our grief rather than seeking out futile and expensive ways to rid ourselves of it. We can begin the deeply personal exploration of what keeps *you* regular. Certain environments, activities and food can either support or impede your body's natural cycles of digestion—some help to keep you regular, whereas others may lead to diarrhea, constipation, cramping, or bloating. Grief is no different. There are environments, activities, and people that will keep you regular, and environments, activities and people that will clog you up. The goal should never be to "recover" or "get over" your grief. The goal should be to understand that grief is an innate, natural mechanism that will accompany you for the rest of your life, always with the sole, singular purpose of keeping you alive. Just like breathing and eating, you will grieve for as long as you live. Learning how your body mourns best; learning what feels good to it and what does not, what impedes its natural cycle and what supports it—these are the questions worthy of your time and exploration.

The understanding of grief as a biological imperative helps us to see how misguided our culture's current pathological orientation to grief is. We would never see the need to eat, drink, or poop as human pathology. We would never tell a person who is breathing that they need to seek psychological intervention in order to rid themselves of their need for oxygen. Yet over and over again, we see even the most well-meaning of people suggest interventions to help people recover, move on, or let go of their grief. A quick Google search will yield endless amounts of people, providers, and authors who promise the right model, modality, or solution to rid you of this apparent affliction. For the right amount of money, you too can be free from the inconvenience of grief. But what if after you've maxed out your time, resources, and capacity, you find that you are still grieving? What if you find that despite their promises and words, you are still impacted even after all these years? Well then, my friend, they will say that *you* are the problem; *you* are the pathology. They will say that your ongoing grief is a disorder, and you will be referred to yet another endless list of people, providers, and authors who will happily take more of your money to cure you of this, too.

I am not asking that you like your grief. I am not asking that you embrace or accept it. You are allowed to protest and tantrum and wish things were very, very different. You are allowed to miss the person you were before grief came in and took up permanent residence inside of you. You are allowed to hate your grief, despise it, and even choose to dismiss or ignore it for long stretches at a time. I am not asking you to be grateful for your grief or to seek out the lessons it has taught you. I would never ask such things. What I am asking you to consider is that nothing is wrong with you *for* grieving. The only thing the presence of grief demonstrates is that you are human, and as a human, you attached, and that attachment was severed. Full stop. That's it. Grief is simply the evidence that you are a human being having a human experience.

One of the most common questions I receive is "How do I help someone who is grieving?" As I'm sure you may have inferred by now, I personally do not use the language of help. I don't believe that grief requires help, intervention, or interference of any kind. In fact, quite to the contrary, I have witnessed repeated experiences throughout my life and career where well-intentioned help, intervention, and interference have only served to add further pain, suffering, and isolation to an already fraught experience. What I do believe in full-heartedly is support. Two of my favourite definitions of support are as follows:

1. to bear all or part of the weight of; hold up
2. to endure bravely

The words "help," "interference," and "intervention" all imply that there is someone who offers the help, interference, or intervention, and someone who requires the help, interference, or intervention. This creates a false dichotomy: The grieving person is no longer seen as the one with the expertise, knowledge, or wisdom of their own experience. It implies that the person outside of the experience, the one who is not having or living the experience, somehow knows better and can see more clearly than the one to whom it is happening. As already established, the person helping often does not have any specific education, training or expertise from which to be offering this help. When I think of the word "support"—to endure bravely—we are suddenly in a different reality. We are in a reality where both the grieving person and those who love and care for them are being asked equally to endure bravely. They are being asked together to bear the weight and hold up what cannot be borne alone. No one is being asked to deny their experience of grief; instead, we acknowledge its everlasting presence and offer to do our part to help shoulder the load.

When I ask people to tell me what sorts of things help keep their digestive systems regular, I am eagerly met with a variety of answers, including but not limited to fruits, vegetables, fibre, water, and movement. When I then proceed to ask what sorts of things help to keep their attachment systems regular, I am most often met with blank stares and silence. Because we don't think of grief as an inherent biological function, we have not been taught the same information on, nor spent the same amount of time learning about, what keeps us fluid and regular when it comes to our grief. Just as things like water, movement, fruits, and vegetables support our digestive system, there are a number of things that support our attachment systems in order to keep our grief metabolizing smoothly.

As far back as we can trace, human beings have been using a combination of community, storytelling, movement, and sound to metabolize the inevitable and continuing losses experienced across our life spans.

It serves to reckon that if attachment is necessary for our survival—meaning we need one another in order to survive—then the reminder of, and the need for, existing attachments would never be more critical than they would be following a loss. Perhaps more than ever, this would be the time our attachment system would need to be reminded—repeatedly and consistently—that we have not been left alone. I want to be clear that when I speak of community, I do not mean that people who are grieving need to be continuously surrounded by people. Quite to the contrary, bereaved people may need a tremendous amount of time alone, and at rest, to allow the body to begin the massive task of digesting and metabolizing the grief they are experiencing. The role or function of the community is to be present to, and for, the grieving person so that they may access the time, space, capacity, and resources required for mourning. Below are some suggestions for practical, ongoing ways you can support someone in your life who is grieving.

- Walk their dog or offer pet care.
- Take out their garbage, recycling, and compost.
- Drop off bags of groceries and household essentials (toilet paper, paper towels, garbage bags etc.)

- Shovel snow, rake leaves, water gardens, mow lawns.
- Clean their home and/or do their laundry.
- Bring in mail
- Drive them to and from appointments.
- Refill prescriptions.
- Send gift cards for food delivery services.
- Purchase gift certificates for in-home cleaning services.
- Bring over meals in pre-portioned, freezable containers.
- Take vehicles in for oil changes and seasonal maintenance (snow tires, etc.)
- Arrange carpool for children (i.e. school pick up and drop off, extracurricular activities, etc.)

Community, and the kind of community that is most beneficial for people who are grieving, must be composed wisely and with great discernment. I often say that there are two requirements that one must demonstrate to be worthy of such an invitation: humility and a firm belief that you cannot possibly understand someone's experience of loss better than they can. After Diane died, it was a rare, and therefore deeply welcomed occurrence for me, to meet other young adults who had experienced a similar loss. There was nothing quite like looking into the eyes of someone else who knew in their cells what experiencing a loss at that particular age was like. It was almost as if we had our own shared language—a deep knowing and understanding that instantly connected us. At a time when so much of my energy was lost in translation, being seen and heard by someone who spoke the same language was the most welcome balm for my tired and weary heart. The same can be said for folks with a shared identity or lived experience. There are times when BIPOC need to be in spaces that are free of the white gaze, when 2SLGBTQIA+ folks need to be in Queer-only spaces, and when chronically ill and disabled folks need to be in spaces free of ableism and all its harmful, unsolicited advice. Similarly, the bereaved would also do well finding spaces where they can be amongst their own. If you are a motherless daughter, find other motherless daughters. If you are someone who has experienced perinatal loss, find the others whose babies did not come home. If you are someone whose loss is ongoing and always present like those who are chronically ill or disabled, find your spoonies and hold them close. We need each other to survive. Truly. Find your people. They're out there, and they need you just as much as you need them.

Storytelling is universal to the human experience. All humans, across all cultures, tell stories. Some of the earliest evidence of stories comes from cave drawings found in Lascaux and Chauvet, France. These drawings date as far back as thirty-two thousand years ago (UNESCO). Although it is impossible to prove, it has been suggested that storytelling developed not long after the development of language itself. Studies in phonemic diversity place the origins of modern language in the range of fifty to one hundred and fifty thousand years ago, around the time of speciation of homo-sapiens (Perreault and Mathew). Stories help us to make sense and meaning of the things that have happened to us; they provide structure in a random and unpredictable world. Stories can also be a window into the lives and experiences of others. They allow us to understand and empathize with those whose life experiences may be vastly different from our own. Storytelling can support bereaved people in exploring the often tragic and unjust nature of life. Perhaps most importantly, storytelling has the power to remind us that we are not alone, that each of us comes from a long line of ancestors who too attached and lost. Each one of us an heir to a rich and enduring legacy, descendants of humans who—despite harrowing odds—somehow found their way through.

When we think of our digestive systems, we understand that not all meals are able to be consumed and digested equally or at the same rate. A seven-course French tasting menu is going to require a lot more time and energy to consume and digest than a small bowl of bone broth. The same can be said for the events we experience throughout our lives. One of the ways I see Western-based counselling and psychotherapeutic practices cause harm is when practitioners make the false assumption that repetition equals pathology. I have heard many colleagues speak poorly and harshly of clients who return each week repeating the same stories, sharing the same struggles and grievances. It is often when the practitioner begins to feel insecure or frustrated about their own skills due to their client's perceived lack of progress that the following words and statements begin to make an appearance: "My client is stuck; they are in denial; I don't think they are willing or ready to do the work; they don't want to change; they are choosing to remain in a perpetual state of bereavement/dissatisfaction," etc. The practitioner begins to create false narratives about their client's resilience, willingness, and capacity stemming from their feelings of ineffectiveness. They project their own equally inaccurate sense of incompetency onto their clients, and the therapeutic relationship begins to break down. Not all meals digest with the same ease or at the same rate, and so is true for loss. Not all losses will metabolize at the same rate or with the same ease. Losing a beloved elder at the end of a long, fulfilling life is not the same experience as someone who has experienced the death of a loved one due to police brutality and racial violence. We need not subscribe to our culture's false hierarchy of loss. I believe fully and wholeheartedly that all loss is valid, as is all grief, but this does not mean that they are the same. To not acknowledge difference is to enact harm. We have the capacity to validate and acknowledge all kinds of loss without needing to pretend that they are the same. Some of us are from communities that experience loss at significantly disproportionate rates. Some communities experience loss so frequently that there is no opportunity to begin metabolizing one loss before another one occurs. Some of us come from communities where we were born into the experience of intergenerational and epigenetic loss—communities that cannot remember or conceive of a time when life and loss were not mutually exclusive to one another. Asking or expecting people to metabolize their loss at the same rate as people who have had vastly different lived experiences is an act of violence. Not everything that happens in life is digestible, and to pretend otherwise is to be willfully ignorant. We don't all heal or overcome; not all grief can be metabolized. It is not true that all of us make it, so if you have the great honour and privilege of finding yourself across from someone as they begin to tell you their story, you have two jobs and two jobs only: listen and believe them. Do not interrupt with your opinions or unsolicited advice. Do not tell them that you know how they feel and then centre yourself and your own experiences of loss in their story. Do not assume that you could possibly see, know, or understand their experience better than they can. *Just listen and believe them.* Believe that what they are saying is true and believe that they know themselves and their own experience better than you ever could. Should it get repetitive, and it seems as though they are rigorously chewing on a particular part of their story, remember that not all things can be swallowed, and instead of judging them or checking out, listen even more closely for the piece that cannot be digested, and silently extend to them the grace and compassion they so deeply deserve.

Human beings have been innately employing the benefits of movement and sound as far back as we can trace. Many cultures have long-standing rituals, ceremonies, and practices—both in times of celebration and in times of loss or transition—that incorporate elements of movement and sound. These cultures seem to have an inherent knowing and understanding of how movement and sound support the body's natural metabolization of grief. Similar to how movement and hydration are key elements in keeping our digestive systems on track, movement and sound are equally essential to keeping our attachment systems flowing regularly. In her book, *Trauma Stewardship*, author Laura Van Dernoot Lipsky recounts her discovery of these long-standing practices from conversations she had with psychiatrist Dr. Bessel van der Kolk:

> Bessel van der Kolk worked with Bishop Tutu in South Africa, and he says there are a variety of ways that humans manage trauma, and in most of the world it's through bodily movement, often dancing or other things music related. One small portion of the world where trauma is not dealt with that way is Northwest Europe. The tradition there is alcohol. Van der Kolk talked about when he'd attend the Truth and Reconciliation Commission and they'd open up the hearings in the mornings, and it'd start with Tutu singing and then everybody singing, and then they'd dance and after a period then they'd stop, hear a few witnesses sharing unbearable stories, and then Tutu would sing again and dance and then take a few witnesses so that at each step they were managing until they couldn't bear it or hold it any longer, and then they'd sing again and do some sort of bodily movement. (357–58)

When I hear the story of how beautifully and thoughtfully Reverend Desmond Tutu led his people through the painful, difficult process of reconciliation, I am angered at how poorly and unskillfully we treat our bereaved. What seems so clear to me is how much Reverend Tutu wanted the experience of reconciliation to be reparative for his people rather than retraumatizing. For hundreds of years his people, the South African people, have been using forms of movement (dancing) and sound (music, singing, drumming) to metabolize the loss and trauma they've endured. One particular form of dance, pantsula, is a South African dance form that originated in Johannesburg during apartheid, coming to prominence through the student uprisings of the 1970s and 80s. People of various marginalized communities were able to come together and collectively express their shared experiences of apartheid (Drummond-Smith and Saunders). Reverend Tutu used a combination of community, storytelling, movement and sound to ensure that his people would be well supported throughout this difficult process. Tutu made certain that his people would together bear the weight of what they had experienced, ensuring their ability to continue enduring on, bravely, together.

When I think of what we do with our bereaved—how we send them off on their own to professionals who have no mandated education or training in grief and loss; professionals who are unable to disclose whether they are one of your own, whether they too have ever experienced this kind of loss; how we then demand that they share their most personal and intimate stories with this stranger, share in complete isolation without any community and without any movement or sound to metabolize what they've shared; and how we send them back out into the world again, alone, sixty minutes later with no follow-up or aftercare—I am aghast that we dare to call this therapeutic. I am equally appalled at how we then turn around and pathologize the bereaved when this feeble and meagre approach fails to produce the results we claimed it would. It makes me weep at the harm being done to those who are at their most vulnerable. I believe we can do *so* much better. I know we can. We must.

I am taking this in, slowly,
Taking it into my body.
This grief. How slow
The body is to realize
You are never coming back.

—Slowly, Donna Masini

Chapter Four

Learning to Live Without

Is It Possible That Humans Can Metabolize Grief without the Interference or Intervention of Paid Professionals?

Just as there are varied and unique ways in which grief manifests, there are equally varied and unique ways in which we metabolize our grief or mourn. For most of us, our dominant ways of metabolizing grief are just as involuntary as grief itself. Western culture has a long-standing and often unconscious bias towards a particular kind of mourning. We are taught both implicitly and explicitly that speaking openly about our feelings and expressing them are the only healthy ways of living with grief. We are often told that if we do not face our experiences and feel our feelings head on, we are then denying, avoiding, or repressing our grief. Traditional talk therapy is often touted as the sole, universal solution to coping with grief effectively. Nothing could be further from the truth. In this chapter, we are going to explore the variety of ways humans metabolize grief and dismantle the myth that feeling and expressing are inherently healthier and more adaptive than other forms of mourning.

The diverse ways people metabolize grief can generally fall into three categories. There are those whose primary way of metabolizing grief is cognitive, those whose primary way of metabolizing grief is emotional, and those whose primary way of metabolizing grief is physical. I want to emphasize the word "primary," meaning that most of us have a dominant way that we metabolize grief. This does not mean that we do not ever dabble in or experience other ways of mourning; it simply means that most of us have a main point of entry from where we begin.

For people whose primary way of metabolizing grief is cognitive, this could look like a variety of things, including but not limited to researching, reading, thinking, and/or writing. During an experience of loss, some people will immediately open their laptops and Google everything they can on the subject matter. Others will collect and gather information, order all the books, and read all the articles. They will seek out online communities of others who have experienced something similar and read about their experiences. Others still will spend hours quietly thinking and processing all that they have learned. Some cognitive mourners may also metabolize grief through writing or journalling. For people who mourn cognitively, the process of gathering information and understanding what it is they are going through supports their metabolization of grief.

For those whose primary way of mourning is emotional, this can look like a lot of big feelings (e.g., crying, raging, and/or experiencing anxiety). It can look like reminiscing, memorializing, and taking part in a variety of mourning rituals both public and private. People who mourn emotionally tend to find great comfort in sharing their stories and connecting with others who have similar lived experiences (e.g., attending support groups). For these people, the sharing and expression of feelings support their metabolization of grief.

Finally, for those whose primary way of mourning is physical, this can look like a whole lot of doing (e.g., building things, making lists, organizing meal trains, and/or attending to things like estates or taxes). These are often the people who, in times of loss, get things done. They can put their heads down and get to work. Less obvious ways of physical mourning can include organizing, cleaning, purging, labelling, and decluttering. A telltale sign for me that I am in a moment of grief is when I undoubtedly find myself on my hands and knees cleaning out the fruit and vegetable bins at the bottom of my fridge. The cleaner my house looks, the more broken my heart. For some, mourning physically can look like movement, (e.g., working out, running, hiking, walking, and playing sports). For people who mourn physically, it is the act of doing and moving that supports their metabolization of grief.

The important thing to note about the diverse ways that human beings mourn and metabolize grief is that there is no one way that is inherently superior to another. No one way of metabolizing grief is inherently better or healthier. The most important thing is not *how* one is metabolizing their grief but that one *is* metabolizing their grief. The person who is going to talk therapy every week is not doing something that is inherently healthier than the person who is going for a jog at 6:00 a.m. The person who is attending a weekly support group is not inherently a more skilled mourner than the person who hasn't left their bed—and their laptop—for weeks. Not all people, or bodies, metabolize grief the same way. The best way to metabolize grief is to metabolize it *your* way.

It can sometimes be challenging to decipher what your dominant way of mourning or metabolizing grief is. When I was in graduate school, I had a student placement at a community-based bereavement support agency here in Toronto. While I was there, I was invited to participate in its bereavement volunteer training program. It was in that training that I met a dear mentor of mine. She was leading an exercise with the group about the diverse ways that people mourn, and she asked us each to place ourselves in the quadrant we felt most represented our dominant style of mourning. I was at a loss. As I looked around at the options, I thought to myself, "Well, I do cry sometimes, and I did go to a bereavement support group after Diane died. I do tend to clean and organize when I'm feeling overwhelmed with grief." There was a part of each quadrant that spoke to me, so narrowing in was proving to be quite the challenge. My mentor could see my struggle and gently placed her hand against my back. She looked at me with much tenderness and grace and said, "We all do all things. However, what I see in front of me is someone who after losing the person they loved most in the world decided to leave behind their career and everything they had ever known to pursue a master's degree in grief and loss. I see someone who needed and wanted to understand everything they possibly could about what they were experiencing. I see someone who consumed and learned absolutely everything they could about grief. I see someone who is seeking to comprehend, and master, this beast that has come in and changed everything that once was." It was then, and only then, that I was able to see how much my academic pursuits *were* my primary means of mourning. It was only in the gentleness of her words that it became clear to me that my dominant way of mourning was cognitive. I share this story to illustrate that having a dominant way of mourning does not mean it is your *only* way of mourning. Emotional grievers get things done; physical grievers have feelings; but your dominant way of mourning will be your entry point. Those who metabolize grief emotionally will need to have the space to experience and express their feelings before they can get to their list of tasks. Similarly, those who metabolize grief physically will need to move before they can access or express their feelings. Sometimes it is in the doing or movement itself that allows space for the feelings or thoughts to emerge. As a cognitive mourner, I need to understand intellectually what is happening before I can clean my house and well before I am able to have a good cry. It is worth noting that for many cognitive and physical mourners, our preference will still be to have and express our feelings privately or in the presence of a cherished, select few.

Six years ago, I was working in a rural residential hospice in Southern Ontario. While there, I had the great honour of meeting a special woman who for the sake of anonymity has asked to be called B. At the time, B was in her forties, and she had two children who were aged twelve and seven. Her husband had died of cancer at the hospice, and she was coming to see me for weekly bereavement support. In one of our sessions, she told me that she was quite worried about her twelve-year-old daughter. When I asked her what in particular was concerning her, she shared with me that her daughter wasn't talking about her dad much and that she had not seen her cry or express much emotion since his death. She then shared with me that every day after school, her daughter would come home, go into the kitchen, and begin to organize the pantry. She would go through and match up the Tupperware bottoms to their lids, and place boxed and bagged items into containers. She would then label items and organize the shelves according to similar themes and uses. Due to our culture's bias towards talking and expressing feelings, my client was understandably concerned about her daughter's behaviour. The thing is her daughter was simply someone who best metabolized her grief by doing, in this case by organizing and cleaning. She was a physical mourner. My client was an emotional mourner who best metabolized her grief by sharing and expressing her feelings. Cleaning out the pantry would be no more beneficial to my client than coming to see me would have been for her daughter. It was simply a difference as opposed to a cause for concern. Both were grieving, and both were metabolizing their grief in the way that was best for them. Sometimes the most loving thing we can do is to simply let someone be—to give someone the space to metabolize their grief in the way that feels right for them, free of judgement, and free of bias or comparisons. No two losses are the same and no two people are the same. What worked for you is not a blueprint for what will work for someone else. Only when we truly understand and appreciate that there is not a morally or psychologically superior way to metabolize grief does the possibility of skillful grief support emerge.

A well-known bit of grief theory that explores the question of whether gender impacts how we cope with grief can be found in Kenneth Doka and Terry Martin's book *Grieving Beyond Gender: Understanding the Ways Men and Women Mourn*. In their work, Doka and Martin elaborate on their conceptual model of "styles or patterns of grieving"—a model that has generated both research and acceptance since the publication of the first edition in 1999. In the original book, as well as in the revision, Doka and Martin explore the different ways that individuals grieve. While I personally do not, and cannot, support the binary presentation of gender in their work, I do believe that their introduction of intuitive and instrumental grief styles (or to use my language, ways of mourning and/or metabolizing grief) is worth sharing here.

Intuitive grievers are those whose grief manifests in strong affective reactions. For intuitive grievers, their expression of grief mirrors their internal feelings, meaning their internal landscape is most often congruent with their external expressions of grief. If an intuitive griever feels sad, they will express that sadness externally. If an intuitive griever feels impatient, they will express that impatience externally. There is not a lot of guesswork involved with intuitive grievers. For them, metabolizing grief involves a significant amount of expressing and exploring feelings. A fun way that I like to think of intuitive grievers is by remembering that they prefer to mourn eyeball to eyeball. These are the folks who want to be seen in their grief. These are the folks who thrive in bereavement support groups where they can explore, express, and share their feelings with others. These are folks who find more traditional forms of individual grief support useful. These are folks who simply need someone to sit across from them and ask, "How are you *really*?" Then off to the races they will go. I often affectionately refer to intuitive grievers as self-cleaning ovens. If given the proper space in which they can safely express and explore their feelings, they will metabolize their grief all on their own. They will not need interference, intervention, or unsolicited advice. They simply need you to show up, listen, and let them do their thing.

Instrumental grievers are those who metabolize grief primarily via physical or cognitive means. For instrumental grievers, the expression of their grief will either be cognitive or behavioral in nature. This means that their external expression of grief will often be incongruent with their internal landscape. For instrumental grievers, metabolizing grief involves a great deal of either thinking (cognitive) or doing (physical). Because so much of their mourning occurs either internally and privately (thinking) or through action (doing), those around them do not always receive the same external cues that intuitive grievers offer. If I were riding the subway and the person next to me was crying, I would have an external cue that something was troubling them. However, if I were out walking my dog and the person next to me was out for a jog, there would be no external cue that lets me know they are hurting. This can often lead to people making inaccurate assumptions about instrumental grievers. It is not uncommon for intuitive grievers to create false narratives about instrumental grievers being in denial simply because their style of metabolizing grief looks so different from their own. Whereas intuitive grievers like to mourn eyeball to eyeball, instrumental grievers prefer to mourn either shoulder to shoulder or back-to-back. This might look like going for a walk, run, or hike together. It may look like a leisurely car ride on a Sunday afternoon or cooking a meal next to one another in the kitchen. It could look like sitting back-to-back on a blanket, each one of you nose deep in a book of your choosing. It could look like lying down next to one another listening to the same podcast. It may be true that while on the hike or in the car the conversation naturally turns towards grief and thoughts or feelings are shared, but it is equally possible that just being there next to an instrumental griever in complete silence is enough. These folks metabolize grief through action or thinking, so more often than not, just letting them do what they need to do—free of judgment and assumptions—is the most effective way of offering your support.

In my family, my daughter is an intuitive griever. When she is grieving, all I need to do is scoop her up, look her straight in the eye, and let her unleash in my arms as I witness her pain. She will cry and yell and express all of the things. Within approximately thirty minutes, she will naturally fatigue, and that particular wave of grief will have been metabolized.

Depending on the time of day, she will then either fall asleep or carry on feeling lighter and more resourced than before. She simply needs her pain to be witnessed and held before she is ready to carry on. My stepson is a highly instrumental griever. Very rarely will he express his feelings outwardly. He is a deep thinker and a voracious reader. If I want to connect with him, I will almost always suggest an activity based on our shared interests. We are both foodies who love to explore new cuisines, so more often than not I will invite him out for a meal and have him pick out a restaurant of his choosing. Sometimes before our meeting, I will send him an article or a link to a podcast that I think he will like and ask him to read it/listen to it before our date. It is almost always in the car ride over, as we sit shoulder to shoulder, where I will ask him his opinion on what he's read or listened to, and it is there that the conversation and connection begin. It is through the process of sharing thoughts and ideas over a shared activity and interest that I offer my support and care. Both kiddos metabolize grief and experience connection in wildly different ways, but one is not better than the other; they are just different. It is in my ability to offer the kind of care that best supports their individual needs that makes the support effective.

My preferred style of metabolizing grief is relevant when seeking out support for myself; however, it is entirely irrelevant when offering support to others. It is very important for you to be able to recognize your preferred methods of mourning so that you can seek out support that will not only feel good to you, but that will equally support your metabolization of grief. Additionally, it is critical that you are aware of your preferred methods of mourning so you can be aware of the biases you will likely have as a result and keep them in check accordingly.

What I have seen happen over and over again throughout my career, is well-meaning, intuitive grievers (often support practitioners themselves) aggressively advocating for instrumental grievers to seek out and participate in bereavement support programs that only support the needs of intuitive grievers. They do this without understanding the harm it does to those who do not metabolize grief through the expression and exploration of feelings. Of course, it makes sense that after a one-hour traditional grief support session or a bereavement support group, intuitive grievers experience great comfort and relief. For them, they have just spent time metabolizing grief and as such, they leave feeling more resourced and more spacious. For instrumental grievers who metabolize grief by thinking, doing, or both, they would have spent the same time accumulating *more* grief in their minds and bodies (often from listening to the experiences of others or being forced to share their own) without any means to metabolize it. Therefore, they leave the experience feeling more agitated and overwhelmed than they did when they arrived. Consequently, they now must spend however much time outside of the support session metabolizing all of the grief they have just accrued to return to their baseline. It would be no different from an instrumental griever—who metabolizes grief through physical activity—showing up each morning at 6:00 a.m. to an intuitive griever's home while enthusiastically yelling, "Rise and shine! Up and at 'em!" assuming that the intuitive griever will experience the same kind of spaciousness that they do following a run. To the intuitive griever, it would likely seem insensitive and inappropriate to show up at their house at 6:00 a.m. demanding that they participate in physical activity, given that they are in mourning. The point is that often the activity itself is neutral; one is not better or healthier. It only matters that you are participating in the activities that support you in metabolizing your grief. When I am leading grief literacy training sessions, I will often use the example of a car ride to illustrate this point further. If you were to invite an instrumental griever for a Sunday drive, you could do the whole car ride listening to music, discussing a podcast, or even simply sitting in complete silence, and the instrumental griever would likely leave the experience feeling both connected and supported. If you were to invite an intuitive griever on the same car ride and never explicitly ask them about or discuss their loss, they would leave the experience feeling hurt, disconnected, and agitated. The car ride itself is the same; it is neutral. What is relevant is how the person experiences the car ride. Do not ask yourself to be something you are not, and please do not ask others to be what they are not. If you need to alphabetize your pantry—do it. If you need to stay in bed for weeks and months at a time crying until your sheets are soaked through—do it. If you need to ride your bike farther than you thought your legs could carry you—do it. All is welcome. *You* are welcome.

IN PRACTICE

My first job out of graduate school was at a community-based hospice an hour or so east of Toronto. I was young and green, and to this day I remain so profoundly grateful to all of those who shared their stories with me so I could learn and do better. One client—and one story—in particular sticks out to me as being a crucial and integral part of my own learning and development. With my client's permission, I will share her story with you here. At the time of our first meeting, my client was in her early fifties. Her adolescent son had recently died by suicide. She was coming to me because of the challenges she was experiencing with her husband since their son's death. She was someone who felt very comfortable talking about her son, both his life and death. She loved having photos of him around the house and sharing her memories of him with others. Her husband was someone who had not spoken of his son since the day of his funeral. He continually removed photos and mementos of him from around the house. He did not acknowledge his son's life, or death, verbally in any way. She was worried that her husband was isolating himself, and she was beginning to resent how he was responding. She did not feel like he was grieving or honouring their son. She questioned whether she loved their son more than he did, and she asked herself if she could stay with someone who seemed so cold and uncaring. When I asked her what her husband did with his days, she shared with me that they had a small barn on the back of their property and that he would spend most of his days from sunrise to sunset there. He had not returned to work since his son's death and therefore spent his time alone at the edge of their property. I asked her if she knew what he was doing in the barn, and she said that just before their son's death, they had purchased an old boat, and she imagined he was likely tinkering with that. One day, about three months after we had initially begun seeing one another, my client came in, and everything about her looked different. Her face was relaxed; she appeared noticeably less agitated. We sat down, and she immediately told me that a few days before our meeting, her husband had come up unexpectedly from the barn for lunch. When he came into the house, he asked her if she

> would join him in the barn as there was something he would like to show her. My client agreed, and after they ate, she made the long walk to the back of the property with her husband. When she entered the barn, she saw something that stunned her and instantly moved her to tears. There right in front of her, almost unrecognizable to her, was that dingy old boat transformed into a thing of such magnificent beauty with her son's name painted across the side. In that instant, everything became clear to her. Her husband had been just as devasted by their son's death as she was. He loved his boy just as much as she did. He spent every moment of every day, from sunrise to sunset, mourning his son. He simply was not one to put his experience into words. Instead, he poured all of his love and all of his grief into the construction of this breathtaking memorial to his son.

Our society's unfounded bias towards emotional expressions of loss is not the only misconception that impedes our ability to metabolize grief. Another myth that hinders how we mourn is the myth of closure. In 2012, Nancy Berns, a sociologist at Drake University, gave a lecture at a TEDx event in Des Moines, Iowa, titled "Beyond Closure." In it, Berns identifies closure as a fabricated concept. She says, "Closure seduces us. We want that. So, businesses use closure to sell products. Closure's the sizzle. The funeral industry promises closure. The grief and the memorialization industries promise closure. Those selling autopsy services, private DNA profile kits, wrongful death attorneys, they're promising closure if we buy their products and services" (Berns 5:47–6:15).

In her latest book, *Closure: The Rush to End Grief and What It Costs Us*, Berns explores how closure has been applied widely in popular media and how the idea has been appropriated as a political tool to sell products and services (3). When we spend all of our time, capacity, and resources seeking closure, we refrain from developing the skills needed to support the metabolization of grief across our lifespan.

In stark contrast to the myth of closure, more recent, evidence-based grief theories reveal that grief is something that we will experience and metabolize across the entirety of our lives. One of my favourite bits of grief theory demonstrating this concept is found in the work of Dr. Therese

Rando, a psychotherapist and grief counsellor who in the early 1990's coined the term "STUG." STUG is an acronym for a sudden (or subsequent), temporary, upsurge of grief. A STUG is used to describe an intense upsurge of grief that occurs unexpectedly and episodically throughout the life of a bereaved person. I remember so clearly an experience I had about seven or eight years following Diane's death when I went to get groceries one evening after work. It was an entirely ordinary day, and as I turned down one of the aisles, there was something about the fluorescent lighting and the completely mundane nature of going grocery shopping on a Tuesday evening that simply wrecked me. My throat tightened, and hot tears immediately filled my eyes. My heart physically hurt, and I had to leave the store and head home empty-handed. It was not her birthday. It was not nearing the anniversary of her death. It was not a special holiday. It was the sudden, unexpected awareness of myself grocery shopping on a completely ordinary Tuesday evening while she was still dead that unravelled me. There was nothing I could have done to predict or prevent it. There was nothing specifically triggering. It was simply a sudden, temporary, upsurge of grief, a STUG, on an entirely ordinary Tuesday evening. What I love so much about this concept is how it validates and normalizes these experiences of grief across time. The "S" speaks to the fact that these experiences are sudden. Modern psychotherapists love to talk about triggers, the implication being that if you simply do the work of identifying and exploring your triggers, you can then make a life for yourself where you will no longer experience them. This might be useful for avoiding crowds or loud noises, but it is going to fall woefully short when it comes to grief. The very fact that these STUGs are sudden in nature acknowledges that they can, and will, occur both unexpectedly and unavoidably. The "T" reminds us that these episodes are temporary. When you are in the early years of grief, it can feel like you are experiencing one STUG after another after another, so much so that entire days and weeks can feel like one long STUG. The "T" helps us to remember that we will not get stuck in one forever. Despite their intensity, the frequency and the duration of these experiences will diminish over time, allowing us a moment to catch our breath and rest before the next one arrives. The "UG" offers us the language to name the experience we are having. When in an upsurge of grief, we must name it as such. You are not falling apart. You are not having a meltdown or breaking down. You are a human being who at one point in time involuntarily attached to something or someone that was of great value to you, and your attachment was severed. The presence of a STUG is not representative of you being stuck. It is not representative of you not having done your grief work. It is not symbolic of some kind of personal failing, liability, or weakness. It is simply evidence that you are human. That's it. You are a human being. Human beings attach, attachments are severed, and grief ensues. None of this is unique, and none of this is optional. What Rando's contribution illuminates is that grief remains ever present across our lifespans. Grief does not resolve or complete, but this does not mean it remains constant or fixed. In parenting, what a newborn requires from their parent is different than what a toddler or adolescent may need; and in grief, what you experience in the early years is different from how that same loss is experienced decades down the road. Although the occurrence of these STUGs will continue across our lifespan, the frequency with which they occur and the amount of time they last do shift over time. What does all of this mean? Well, to me, it confirms that if one day I should find myself watching the sunset over the ocean, after a long and plentiful life, and the grief swells up because the beauty of it overcomes me, and I wish so much she had lived to see the entirety of what a life could be, I will know in my bones that not only is this okay but that I have carried the torch of her memory as brightly and bravely as I could.

June 27, 2018

The day you were born. And I'm so glad you were. It has meant so much to me. Your life.

At work recently, I've been feeding this elderly man. And we go ever so slowly. One mouthful and then another. Some water from a straw. Swallow. Another bite. Repeat. Ever so slowly, nothing else to do, nowhere else to be. It's quiet and ever so intimate. And it has reminded me of when that was you and I. Day after day, just you and I up in that white bedroom, watching the branches of the oak tree sway outside the window. Tomato soup. Soda crackers. Mustard poultice. I remember you told me, "This is the first time in my life there isn't any wind, you know?" I've done the same thing recently. In every possible way I can, I have cut out the wind. And what remains is a kind of stillness. It's what I feel when I'm feeding this man, and walking to work each morning as I pass the very building you died in, and riding the subway studying the faces of strangers wondering about the invisible stories we all carry. Stillness. It's very quiet these days on the inside, and so much is returning to me: the memory of how much meaning I found in those quiet afternoons of laundry and rest, soup and medications carefully laid out, hands held and no wind. I've decided to try it again, to let myself have the kind of life that meant most to me, but this time in the living, with the living.

So, on this day of your birth, I wanted to come here and name that you are still so very much alive in me, all the time, and every day, alive. And that I miss you. I so, so deeply miss you. And also, happy birthday my love. I am so glad you came.

–Rachelle Bensoussan

Chapter Five

Grief as a Chronological Age

An Inquiry of What Childhood Models of Development Can Teach Us about Living with Loss and Supporting Those Grieving

In my many years of practice, I have often found it frustrating that so many prevalent, modern-day grief theories seem to be divided into two camps regarding their intended audiences. One set of theories targets the bereaved, whereas the other targets professionals working with the bereaved. Once again, this only serves to reinforce the false dichotomy between those who are bereaved and those who are "helping" the bereaved. I wanted to create a model, or blueprint, of grief support that both the bereaved and those supporting them could navigate together. I often joke that if I were not a very tired middle-aged parent, I would do a PhD to give this model some kind of socially sanctioned credibility. Thankfully, I have a beautiful wife who challenges my own internalized nonsense that wants to dictate who and what is deemed credible, in addition to reminding me that we have many adventures yet to pursue outside the walls of ivory towers.

Losing my beloved, Diane, at twenty-five shattered my world. I often speak of my life in terms of before and after. There was the person I was before her death and the person I became after it. Plain and simple. Very similar to when one becomes a parent for the first time, you never go back to the person you were beforehand. Even if your baby or child dies, you don't ever get to return to the person you were before their existence was made known and possible. It is important to note that this is neither good nor bad, positive or negative. It simply is. There are things we experience in this world that change us permanently. Certain experiences and events teach us things we would not have otherwise known. There are many parts of my former self that I miss deeply. I miss the girl that did not immediately consider every possible hidden threat when making even the smallest decision. I miss the girl who did not need her loved ones to check in with her at regular intervals. I miss the parent I would have been, the one who would likely have not kept her daughter in a five-point harness well into the third grade, or the one would not have bought her a watch with a built in GPS-tracking device when she was eight. There are also many things I love about the woman I am today. I love the ease at which I can access empathy and understanding for others. I love that people immediately feel safe with me and seen by me, even when they can't necessarily locate why. I love that I let my daughter talk me into staying up well past her bedtime to watch age-inappropriate television while we snuggle in close. I love that I have never prioritized homework or the opinions of others over another round of cards or a poorly timed vacation. I miss welcoming the change in seasons instead of feeling the grief that stirs the moment the leaves begin to turn. I miss the girl who could watch the sunset over the ocean without feeling her throat tighten and burn, the girl who could hold a newborn baby or puppy without tears springing to her eyes because their innocence and vulnerability disarm me. I love the woman who eighteen years later stands along the ocean's edge and loves her kid and writes the book because life is short, and despite overwhelming odds, she lived.

Diane's death changed me in every way a person can be changed. So while I write this at the chronological age of forty-three, my identity as this version of myself is only eighteen years of age. I will be fifty years old when I will finally have been alive—as this version of myself—for as long as I was the person I had been prior to her death. Why does this matter? It matters because understanding myself in this way allows me to treat myself with age-appropriate expectations. While we can love the children in our lives equally, what is appropriate to expect from a preschooler is very different from what is appropriate to expect from a tween. If we were to hold either of them to the other's standard, it would be both ill-fitting and unkind. Using the overlay of childhood development models, I want us to explore the idea of grief having its own chronological and developmental age. If we were to treat ourselves with the age-appropriate expectations of our grief age, rather than that of our chronological age, perhaps we might finally find our way to the understanding and compassion we are so desperately seeking.

As discussed in previous chapters, humans undergo considerable biological, psychological, and emotional changes following loss. If our identities and lives are born anew when our assumptive worlds are shattered, it would help to treat ourselves as the wobbly-legged, deer-in-headlight neonates that we are.

Let's start at the very beginning: infancy. Infancy is the period from birth through the completion of the twelfth month of life (Hedayat) and is characterized as the most rapid velocity of growth of any of the postnatal stages (Bogin). This is an interesting fact because it directly contradicts one of the most prevalent beliefs in our culture: time spent sleeping or resting is unproductive. According to the National Sleep Foundation, infants require fourteen to seventeen hours of sleep per day. Some newborns may sleep up to eighteen or nineteen hours a day. If sleep or rest is unproductive, how can infancy be characterized as the time when the most rapid growth occurs? If you read Chapter Three, you may already know the answer! Much of the rapid growth occurring in infancy is involuntary, meaning it does not require the infant's active participation or consent to occur. What the body and brain need most is for the infant to sleep and rest in order to support the rapid growth and development that is occurring. Similar to a pregnant body in its first trimester, a tremendous amount of sleep and rest are required to support the growth and development of the fetus inside. Sleep and rest are some of the healthiest and most supportive things we can offer our bodies during times of rapid growth and development. This is no different in times of life-altering grief and loss. When someone experiences the shattering of their assumptive world, it requires an enormous amount of growth and development to adjust and adapt to one's rapidly changed reality. We would never shame or judge an infant for sleeping. Most caring adults encourage their infants to sleep the moment they notice them getting fussy or overtired. We scoop them up, cradle them in close, and sing or rock them into a deep slumber. We don't try and talk them into staying awake or encourage them to push through and keep busy. We understand that they have reached a very real limit. We believe it to be in their best interest to be taken somewhere quiet by someone to whom they feel securely attached and rest. Can you imagine a world where bereaved people—particularly in that first year following a loss—were invited to take up rest and sleep whenever needed? Can you imagine a world where grieving folks are not criticized or pathologized for staying in bed all day? A world where they are not judged for needing to collapse and nap by noon or shamed for bowing out early from events. A world where their limits are acknowledged and validated as both worthy and real. A world where everyone around the bereaved offers out the same grace and understanding we offer out so freely to infants. A world where we see the rest they so desperately need as restorative rather than lazy or alarming.

In addition to sleep, infants need to eat, breathe, pee, and poop to survive their infancy. When an infant is being raised by caring adults, no development or milestone is too small to be celebrated. A baby laughs for the first time—the audience cheers! A baby tries a new food—the crowd goes wild! An infant poops after an episode of gassiness—thunderous applause from all! An infant's accomplishments are not held up against the accomplishments of fully grown children. We shower them with praise and adoration for their willingness and efforts alone. We do not criticize infants for crying when hungry or screaming when their diapers are wet. We understand that this is their only way of communicating to us that they have a need. Although it may be unpleasant to listen to, we hear their cries as a request for support—a sign that something is not as it should be and a call to those they need most to come and make things right. I imagine a world where, similar to infancy, the accomplishments of grieving folks are not held up against the ability and capacity of those who are not bereaved. I imagine a world where their willingness and efforts towards survival are met with a standing ovation from those they love most. You got out of bed and brushed your teeth today—the audience cheers! You showered and got the kids out the door with their lunches made—the crowd goes wild! You are eating, breathing, peeing, and pooping—thunderous applause from all! Just as infants deserve to be surrounded by caring adults who enthusiastically praise their every effort, so too do the bereaved.

Starting over in a new and overwhelming reality is scary. One of the ways that infants thrive is through the consistent and reliable attention of caring adults. Babies may have multiple adults with whom they bond; however, most infants have around four to six attachment figures, depending on their experiences of being cared for (KidsHealth NZ). Babies only have a handful of primary attachment figures because their attachment systems are still developing. It will take years before they are ready to manage multiple attachments simultaneously. It does not mean that they can't like or care for multiple people; it simply means that their survival is tied only to a precious few. I see this too in newly bereaved people. Their attachment systems are raw and overwhelmed from their recent loss, and because of this, they are not able to manage multiple attachments successfully. Newly bereaved folks can benefit from the consistent, reliable attention of four to six primary attachments. Again, this does not mean that they don't like or care for many people. It means that, for a time, their survival will likely be tied to the precious few who have proven themselves worthy of the responsibility.

In addition to having a developing attachment system, infants also have developing nervous systems. One of the results of having a nervous system that is still in development is that the system itself can become overstimulated quite easily. Think of an infant brought to a family reunion. The baby is passed around to multiple adults. It sees many new and unfamiliar faces and hears many different voices. Suddenly, they feel afraid and overwhelmed and begin searching for the familiarity and safety of their primary attachments. It doesn't take long for their nervous system to flood and a meltdown to begin. The baby then needs to be returned to the safety of its guardian's arms and taken somewhere quiet to reset. I have seen this same scenario play out with newly bereaved people countless times. The bereaved person wants to try going out for brunch with their friends or wants to make an appearance at their work's summer picnic. They show up and for the first while things seem to be okay. At some point, their embryonic nervous system begins to get overstimulated. Someone laughs too loudly, and someone else's voice begins to grate; your colleague won't stop chewing with their mouth open, and before you know it, you are scrambling for the nearest exit as you feel your impending meltdown nearing. Just as an infant would likely do better with a quiet morning visit, newly bereaved folks would do well to plan their encounters accordingly. It is okay to put a time limit on visits or to be picky about locations and times of day. It is okay to say no to things and recognize the limits of your tender nervous system. I invite you to treat yourself with the same kindness and gentleness you would so willingly bestow upon a newborn. Welcome yourself into this new reality calmly and with grace. The road ahead is long, and the path itself is winding. Pace yourself.

Let's move along and take a closer look at toddlerhood. A toddler is a child approximately twelve to thirty-six months old, or one to three years of age. Toddlerhood involves lots of exciting cognitive, emotional, and social developments. The word "toddler" is derived from "to toddle," which means to walk unsteadily. I cannot think of a better way to describe what grieving feels like one to three years following a loss rather than to walk unsteadily. One of the important things I want to stress before we take a deeper look at the developmental needs of toddlers is to emphasize that I am referring to the equivalent time in a bereaved person's life of one to three years following a loss. Not one to three weeks or months but years.

So, what do we know about toddlers? We know that between the ages of one and two, most kids need about eleven to fourteen hours of sleep per day, including one or two daytime naps (Ben-Joseph). At around eighteen months or sometimes sooner, most toddlers condense their two naps into one afternoon nap. A toddler can remain awake for longer than the short windows of their infancy, but they cannot stay awake for more than five hours without needing a nap. Most toddlers can only make it to somewhere around noon before needing to take a well-earned rest. While bereaved people in their second or third years following a loss may feel slightly more capable than they did in that first year, it is not uncommon to tackle a few tasks in the morning only to collapse with exhaustion in the early afternoon.

One of the things that makes toddlerhood such a frustrating time is that there is often a large discrepancy between what one desires versus what one is capable of. A toddler is awake to the world and all its offerings in a way an infant is not. A toddler sees the big kids climbing on the play structure and wants to join in; however, they do not yet have the skill or capacity to do so safely. The discrepancy between what they want to do and are able to do becomes a one-way ticket to tantrum town. This is similar to bereaved folks who may find themselves with a deep desire to rejoin their monthly book club or sign up for a new class with friends but simply do not yet have the ability or capacity to do so. One of the most common things I hear from bereaved people during this time is how sick they are of being where they are, how tired they are of grieving and feeling constantly overwhelmed and exhausted, and how much they want things to be different. If only desire could be translated into capacity, but, alas, it cannot.

A cornerstone of toddlerhood is the struggle to articulate need combined with the inability to emotionally regulate. If I close my eyes, I can vividly remember when my daughter was a toddler. She was always a "spirited" child. I remember one particular morning when she asked me for some grapes. As I happily handed her a bowlful, her face tightened, and her body collapsed to the ground. In a heap of screaming sobs, she shouted, "I wanted grapes in the green bowl not in the blue bowl!" The audacity. Of course, she had not articulated any of this to me previously. I'm not sure if she was aware of her intense need for a green bowl, but when she saw those grapes heading straight for her in a blue bowl, nothing was right in the world. Her inability to predict and articulate her own needs, combined with the inability to regulate her emotions, meant that we spent a lot of time on the floor expressing some very big feelings, very loudly. This, of course, did not last forever. She is now a remarkably articulate twelve-year-old who is somewhat more capable of regulating her emotions and impulses. What she needed most from me during that season of her life was to experience the safety of feeling so out of control next to someone who would stay and love her through it, regardless of how loud, messy, or irrational it may have seemed. She learned that I would remain solid and steady, and that I would always be there on the other side of whatever storm she was in. This is what bereaved people need in their own experience of toddlerhood. They need their people to hold steady. Bereaved folks in the early years following a loss will likely not know what they need until they try it. Often it is in the act of trying itself that we suddenly realize, "No! This is not what I want at all!" The nervous system gets flooded, emotions are overwhelmed, and a meltdown ensues. For both bereaved people and those who love them, please remember that just like toddlerhood, this is a season. It is not who they, or you, will be forever. My recommendation to you—as it was for myself all those many moons ago—is to pull up a comfy cushion, grab a cozy blanket, and settle in. As all storms do, this too shall pass.

The final marker of toddlerhood that I would like to explore is parallel play. Parallel play is a form of socializing in which toddlers play beside one another without trying to influence the other or directly engage. Unlike during infancy, toddlers are ready to branch out beyond their primary attachments. They notice others around them and are curious about engaging. However, as we mentioned above, curiosity or desire does not always equate to the corresponding skill or capacity. Parallel play is the beautiful bridge between the desire to socialize and connect and the skills not yet acquired to sustain such interaction and engagement. In the early years following a loss, there will likely come a time when bereaved people feel ready to take those first, scary steps back out into the world. However, doing so directly may be too much for their systems to manage. Parallel play can be a gentle and fruitful way of testing the waters. Having a trusted friend over to cook a meal side by side can help meet the need for connection without the pressure of keeping up a conversation. A casual drive on a Sunday afternoon listening to music or a podcast can do the same. You could plan a picnic where you both bring something to read while sitting beside each other. There are lots of ways of connecting that do not require talking or crowded, overstimulating environments. When you give yourself permission to meet the needs and desires that accurately correspond to your grief age—rather than those of your chronological age—a world of possibilities emerge. Possibilities for support and connection arise that will likely feel much better to you, in addition to possibilities for understanding and grace that those supporting you might not have otherwise thought to extend.

The Centers for Disease Control recommends that preschoolers (ages three to five) get ten to thirteen hours of sleep per night, a significant amount more than is recommended for the average adult. Preschoolers can imagine and pretend, but they can't always tell what is real and what is not. To them, the scary monsters of their imagination seem real. They are afraid of what might be under the bed or in the closet. Many are afraid of the dark, especially at bedtime. Preschoolers may also be afraid of loud noises like thunder or fireworks. Regressive behaviours are equally common at this stage of development: "When a child is challenged by a new developmental task, [they] are likely to temporarily lose ground in an area recently mastered" (Hurley). I cannot think of a more accurate way to describe the period of three to five years following a loss than "likely to temporarily lose ground in an area recently mastered." The word I want to highlight in that sentence is "temporarily." I have heard so many bereaved people share with me their frustrations and disappointment when they experience what they would call setbacks or a regression. It can be demoralizing and discouraging when you feel like you are right back where you started after so much time has passed, and so much hard work has been done. However, just as with children at this age, regression is not only normal but is part of the process of development itself. We need to take a deep breath, remind ourselves that this is temporary, and trust that the growth and development we have done remain right there inside of us, waiting to be called upon whenever we need it next.

Toddlers experience the world with a false sense of invincibility, unaware of the inherent dangers around them. In the early years following a loss, we too can feel invincible, falsely shouting to the world, "Oh yeah? Try me! I dare you. I've got nothing left to lose." But as we move into years four and five following a loss—just as with preschoolers—the bravado of toddlerhood fades, and we suddenly realize that we are not immune: having one experience of loss does not insulate us from further losses. Similar to how preschoolers begin to become aware of the dangers that may lurk under the bed or in the dark, bereaved people become aware that more life, and more loss, lie ahead. A preschooler's newly acquired anxiety is not dissimilar to the experience of bereaved people at this stage. There is a sudden heightened awareness of the potential dangers around them; a mild yet constant vigilance takes root. They temporarily withdraw from this frightening and perilous world and understand that the things they love most are not promised, and their survival is not guaranteed.

Whenever I share this model of grief, I am inevitably asked, "How do I calculate my grief age if I've had multiple experiences of loss?" Beautiful question. The best way for me to explain this is to use the analogy of parenting. Even though we can all acknowledge that having two children is different from having one and having three children is certainly different than having two, you only ever become a parent for the first time once. The transition from nonparent to parent can only ever occur one time. When you welcome your second child, you are already a parent from when you welcomed your first. While the amount of labour may significantly increase, your identity as a parent already exists. This idea is also true for bereaved people. While I have endured many losses since Diane's death, I only became a bereaved person for the first time once. My assumptive world could only be shattered for the first time once. When calculating your grief age, you may find it easiest to do so by asking yourself, "When did I first become bereaved? When was the first time my assumptive world was shattered?" As mentioned previously, just as in childhood, regressions are normal. Similar to when a toddler welcomes a newborn sibling and reverts back to infant like behaviours, bereaved people will experience a regression of their own when a new loss occurs. So, while your grief age may be ten years old, there will likely be a normal, inevitable regression when you experience subsequent losses.

Using the overlay of childhood development as a means of understanding and orienting to ourselves and others differently, we can begin to ask ourselves two very important questions:

1. How appropriate have your expectations of yourself been given your current grief age?
2. How appropriate have your expectations of others been given their grief age?

One of the things I have done myself, and continue to suggest to those I am supporting, is to find several photos of yourself that align with your current grief age. If your current grief age is three years old, then find photos of yourself as a three-year-old. If your current grief age is eight years old, then find photos of yourself as an eight-year-old. Place these photos in places where you will see them frequently (e.g., on your fridge, the nightstand next to your bed, or as the wallpaper or screensaver on your devices). Having visuals of yourself at your current grief age can serve as a gentle reminder to treat and speak to yourself in an age-appropriate manner. Would you ask a three-year-old, "Why are you so lazy? Why did you sleep through your morning class?" Would you belittle or mock an anxious eight-year-old for feeling overwhelmed in a new setting with new people? Cultivating a relationship with yourself at your grief age, rather than holding yourself to the standards and expectations of your chronological age, can be a powerful and loving tool to add to your toolkit.

November 19, 2017

1. When I was a child, you bought me an extra-large crinkly plush toy that was a combination of a hippo and an elephant for no reason other than I wanted it.

2. Every single year, you would hand knit me a sweater. I remember one had a seal on it, one a unicorn. They were hideous, and I never wore them, but I was always aware of how much love and work went into them, so I always made sure to seem overjoyed when receiving them.

3. You loved to cook and feed me. When I was at your house, I never went hungry.

4. When I slept at your house, I slept on the pullout bed in the den, and it always had red sheets and smelled like the old country, and you would always lie with me and sing to me until I fell asleep.

5. You never tired of telling me the story of how I came to you, how you birthed three sons and always wanted a girl with green eyes and long dark hair, and how you thought God had ignored your prayers – until I was born. You realized you'd been heard all along, and you knew then what it meant to have faith.

6. You never stopped learning. Well into your 80s, you still travelled, took computer courses, and read books.

7. I was your favourite, and you always made sure I knew it.

8. When I came out to you and introduced you to my partner, you embraced us both and never said another word about it.

9. You loved me, and I loved you.

10. This afternoon, peacefully, as you lay sleeping nearly six thousand miles away in a country you called home, your life completed.

As I lie here tonight, my heart broken, I am so proud to have been your granddaughter, to have come from you and your people. Jacqueline Bensoussan, z"l.

–Rachelle Bensoussan

Chapter Six

Why Self-Care Will Not Save Us

A Critique of the Self-Care Movement and How it Further Impedes Our Metabolization of Grief

Many moons ago I made the intentional decision to refrain from using the language of self-care. The term had become so far removed from its original context that I felt I could no longer use it in good faith. I've chosen instead to highlight the true origins of self-care and emphasize the work of its brilliant creator. "Self-care" is a word that has been coopted, commodified, and weaponized against the people and communities to whom it inherently belongs. As Paula Ethans writes:

> The roots of self-care in the anti-oppression struggle are long and deep. For decades, self-care has been a crucial tool for equity-seeking groups. Self-care is linked to pleasure, and for those who consistently have their bodies, lives, and pleasure denied to them—people of color, women, indigent people, and LGBTQ communities—doing things that provide pleasure is indeed radical. In that way, self-care is feminist. It's people standing up for themselves and declaring, I am worthy of love. I require certain basic things and I deserve to be cared for.

The term self-care was originally coined by Audre Lorde, an American writer, womanist, radical feminist, professor, and civil rights activist. She was a self-described "black, lesbian, mother, warrior, poet," who "dedicated both her life and her creative talent to confronting and addressing injustices of racism, sexism, classism, and homophobia" (Poetry Foundation). Before her death in 1992, after being diagnosed with cancer for a second time, Lorde published a book titled *A Burst of Light and Other Essays*. Lorde's infamous quote on self-care appeared in this collection: "Caring for myself is not self-indulgence, it is self-preservation, and that is an act of political warfare" (125).

In Bryony Porteous-Sebouhian's essay "Why acknowledging and celebrating the Black feminist origins of 'self-care' is essential," she reminds us that "For Lorde, self-care wasn't buying a candle, a new herbal tea, or any other form of consumerism, self-care was both the sustenance that sustained her ability to enact change and was in itself a radical act." In the essay "There is No Self-Care without Community Care," Aimaloghi Eromosele shares: "The problem with what I'll call 'new age self-care' is that it can become too capitalistically driven and centered on luxurious pampering that has very little to do with sustainable nurturing and all to do with spending money, which for the communities that actually need the most care, they cannot access!" The whitewashed, highly commercialized version of self-care we currently subscribe to reinforces the very structures that Audre Lorde devoted her life to dismantling.

The solution for structural, institutional, and systemic harm can never be placed on the individual. Accountability for repair must always be placed back onto the structure, institution, or system that caused the harm. Employees do not need another self-care workshop that instructs them on the benefits of sleep, exercise, and a healthy diet. They need work environments that pay them a living wage and labour laws that protect their right to paid time off when they're sick. People need access to affordable housing, healthcare, food, and childcare. The reason the vast majority of people are unable to care for themselves is not because they are unaware of what would make their lives better. It is because they lack access to the resources they would need to make that life possible. Many activists have called for employers to stop using the term "burnout" and have appealed for it to be replaced with the word "exploitation." The term "burnout" focuses on an employee's feelings and asks that they take responsibility for addressing their own feelings of burnout. The word "exploitation" focuses on the practices and policies of the employer as the source of the burnout and demands structural and systemic change instead.

Self-care is considered a core professional competency in social work practice. In its 2021 Code of Ethics, the National Association of Social Workers stated: "Professional self-care is paramount for competent and ethical social work practice. Professional demands, challenging workplace climates, and exposure to trauma warrant that social workers maintain personal and professional health, safety, and integrity." Similarly, self-care is considered a core competency in the field of nursing. A nurse's health can affect the care they provide to patients. The College of Nurses of Ontario's Code of Conduct outlines that nurses must maintain their health and seek help if their health affects their ability to practice safely (15). Both the field of social work and nursing require that their practitioners engage in self-care to ensure that they are practicing safely and mitigating harm.

Another important similarity between nursing and social work is that they are both heavily gendered fields. In the United States, 83.9 per cent of all licensed social workers are women ("Licensed Social Worker Demographics and Statistics"). As of 2021, male nurses comprised only 12 per cent of all registered nurses ("Male Nursing Statistics 2022–2023"). It is curious to me that despite both fields publicly establishing self-care as a requirement for safe and ethical practice, neither has any formal requirements for the organizations that employ these practitioners to provide either the time or the resources needed to access it. If we were to look at this enigma in comparison with a male-dominated field, we would begin to see an appalling set of double standards emerge.

As of 2019, women made up just 22 per cent of all general surgeons, according to the Association of American Colleges, and they were even less represented among specialized surgical fields, such as orthopedic and neurological surgery (Branigin). To do their jobs safely and ethically, surgeons require a great many tools, none of which they are required to provide or pay for out of their own pockets. On any given day, a surgeon will arrive at work and waiting for them—on the hospital's dime—will be an interdisciplinary team, including nurses, anesthesiologists, respiratory therapists, and radiologists. They will have access to a sterile work environment filled with all the surgical equipment and tools they could possibly need. The surgeon's only job is to bring their skills and expertise to the procedure, and their employer, the hospital, takes care of the rest.

In 2021, The Canadian Institute for Health Information listed the average gross annual income for surgeons across all surgical specialties to be $573,586. Comparatively, as of 2024, the average gross annual income for social workers in Canada is $67,830 ("Social Worker Salary in Canada") while their nursing colleagues earn, on average, $74,865 annually ("Nurse Salary in Canada"). Not only is there a massive pay discrepancy between these fields, but what they are required to provide to do their jobs safely and ethically is equally discrepant. The practitioners in the fields dominated by women earn substantially less income yet are expected to access self-care both on their own time and their own dime. The practitioners in the field dominated by men earn eight times the annual income as their nursing and social work colleagues yet are not expected to provide any of the tools required to do their jobs safely and ethically. It almost seems as though the idea of self-care is being used as a scapegoat to remove any accountability and responsibility from the employer for the impact this kind of work has on its employees. Instead of acknowledging the effect working in these fields has and responding accordingly, it is argued that the impact is simply a result of the practitioner not engaging in self-care. Blame is placed back on the individual, thus alleviating responsibility from the organization that employs them.

After years of experiencing the violence of racism, classism, homophobia, and ableism in my professional life, I made an agreement with myself that I would not participate in my own oppression. I understood that I was unlikely to singlehandedly dismantle these systems of harm in my lifetime; however, I refuse to uphold such violence at my own table. This agreement led me to abandon the weaponized version of self-care explored above and begin a different conversation altogether.

Many moons ago, a mentor of mine shared with me a popular comic by Gary Larson. The comic showed a large group of lemmings running on a beach heading straight towards the ocean. At the back of the pack was a single lemming wearing a flotation device. The comic was used as a light-hearted, humorous entryway into a discussion about the inevitable impacts of grief and loss. The lemmings in the comic are all diving head-first into the water. In previous chapters, I used the body—and its many involuntary functions—as an analogy for grief. In this chapter, I would like to focus on water and use one of its inherent paradoxes as another way of understanding and relating to grief and loss. As human beings, water is essential to our survival. We can only survive for approximately three days without adequate hydration, yet it's also true that there are approximately five hundred water-related fatalities each year in Canada (Clemens et al.). The very substance we need to keep us alive can also be the cause of our death. It is not a common occurrence in our lives for something so life-sustaining to simultaneously be so dangerous. I find this paradox a fascinating analogy for grief. I believe grief—when supported and metabolized well—to be one of the most powerful and transformational experiences we as human beings can encounter. I equally believe that when grief is obstructed, impeded, and unable to be metabolized well, the consequences can be fatal. When I think of the potential lethalness of grief, I immediately think of Atatiana Jefferson.

Atatiana Jefferson was a twenty-eight-year-old Black woman who on October 12, 2019, was fatally shot by a police officer inside her home in Fort Worth, Texas while she was playing video games with her nephew. Two weeks after his daughter's funeral, on November 9, 2019, Marquis A. Jefferson, Atatiana Jefferson's father, died at the age of fifty-nine. Marquis Jefferson suffered a cardiac arrest; Atatiana Jefferson was his only child. Family spokesman, Bruce Carter, said "He ultimately just succumbed to, I don't know, I can only say a broken heart. He just never recovered from the grieving process" (qtd. in Maxouris and Silverman). On January 9, 2020, just two months after Marquis' death, Yolanda Carr, Atatiana Jefferson's mother, died as well. She had been hospitalized for weeks due to congestive heart failure. Lee Merritt, family lawyer, shared "We hoped she would pull through. It cannot be underplayed the role Atatiana's death had on Yolanda's health" (NBC News).

It is not true that all of us make it. Some communities experience grief and loss at enormously disproportionate rates due to poverty, racism, homophobia, transphobia, ableism, etc. These communities cannot metabolize their grief from one loss before they are faced with yet another loss and another. These communities often live with the effects of intergenerational and epigenetic losses. Just as it is in the ocean, sometimes the tide is too strong and the waters too chilling to survive.

Grief and loss have an impact. Full stop. You cannot be in the presence of either, whether it be in your personal or professional lives, and not be impacted. When I teach, I often ask, "What would you say if I invited you all to go swimming with me, with the caveat that you cannot get wet? "That's impossible," they reply. "It's not possible to go swimming and not get wet." Exactly! And so it is true with grief. You cannot be in the waters of grief and loss and not be impacted. If you're going to go for a swim, you are going to get wet, and if you're going to be in the presence of grief and loss, you are going to be impacted. The impact is not optional. Professions that weaponize the notion of self-care will tell you that being impacted means you have poor work-life balance. They will tell you that being impacted means you are too emotionally attached and have poor boundaries. They will tell you that being impacted means this work isn't the right fit for you. I call bullshit. We don't stop swimming because we get wet; we make sure we have well-inflated flotation devices nearby and towels waiting for us on the shore for when we need to dry off. It is also true that we don't blindly throw ourselves into the ocean without first assessing the risk. What is the weather forecast? How high are the waves? How strong is the current? When we approach the ocean, we want to do so with a healthy dose of caution, humility, and reverence for the power and potency it contains. We would be wise to do the same when entering the waters of grief and loss. Given that being impacted—or getting wet—is not optional, the question I would like to explore is: How will we stay afloat?

In the Gary Larson comic, all the lemmings appear to be eagerly diving into the water; however, one came prepared. One wise lemming decided to account for the potential risk lying ahead. I would never discourage you from taking a swim in the waters of grief and loss. On the contrary, it is a brave and radical act in a culture that implicitly and explicitly demands that you look away. I want you to swim in all the salty learnings the ocean has to offer. However, I want you to do so safely. I want you to be well prepared for whatever the tides may hold and equipped for all that may emerge from below the surface. I invite you to join me in a little exercise.

Part One

I want you to imagine that you have an invisible flotation device around your body—just like that lone lemming in the comic. This device will support you and keep you afloat regardless of whether the water is smooth or choppy. There are environments, activities, and people that inflate your flotation device, just as there are environments, activities, and people that deflate it. I want you to write out a list of twenty activities that inflate your flotation device. For this exercise, please refrain from adding anything to the list that involves human-to-human interaction (e.g., visiting with family, having brunch with friends, and spending time with your children). Interacting with our furry, four-legged family members is fine, but for today's exercise, we will leave humans out of the equation because most human-to-human interactions involve an exchange of air, meaning that the interactions are reciprocal. In this way, you may receive an inflation of air from the interaction, but some air will also be expelled. It is for this reason I ask that you think of twenty activities that solely inflate your flotation device. You are welcome to include nonreciprocal human-to-human interactions on your list such as massage, therapy, and/or acupuncture. As you come up with your list, notice how easy or difficult it is to come up with twenty items. If you cannot easily find a multitude of ways to inflate your flotation device, this might indicate that you aren't quite ready to go for a swim. It doesn't mean you can't be or won't ever be. It means that there is more work to be done before you are ready to enter the waters safely.

Part Two

Now that you have completed your list of twenty activities that inflate your flotation device, we are ready to move on to part two of the exercise. For part two, I am going to ask that you take your current list of twenty activities and divide them into one of three categories as follows:

- Category one: Any activity on your list that requires both time and resources to access, such as travel, massage, live theatre, guest lectures, live music, therapy, and/or an evening at your favourite restaurant.
- Category two: Any activity on your list that can be accessed within three to five days and requires minimal resources, such as hiking with your dog, playing your guitar, binge-watching your favourite series, gardening, reading, cooking, and baking.
- Category three: Any activity on your list that can be accessed in under fifteen minutes requiring no cost or resources whatsoever, such as meditating, listening to music, singing, having a solo dance

party, reading your favourite piece of poetry or writing, pausing and breathing deeply, and/or making yourself a cup of tea.

After placing each activity into its corresponding category, what do you notice? Are your categories well balanced? Do you have one category that is full while another seems bare? None of this is good or bad; it simply gives you the information you will need to prepare for a safe trip into the water. Allow me to explain each category's purpose and value so you may plan accordingly.

Category One: Imagination and Possibility

For many of us who swim professionally in the waters of grief and loss, perhaps as a social worker, nurse, or mental health practitioner, the activities of category one can feel out of reach. We have already established that women dominate these fields and that these professionals are often overworked and underpaid. Things like massages, travel, or meals at fancy restaurants may seem like a cruel reminder of experiences outside our reach—adventures and experiences that are not meant for us to have. For this reason, I want to be explicitly clear that category one—in the way that I am imagining it—is not a bucket list. It is not meant to be a list of all the things we wish we could access but for very real reasons cannot. Instead, I am asking you to think of category one in the realm of what is possible and not yet able to be known. For this reason, I like to call category one the category of imagination and possibility. In the early years after Diane died, no one could have told me—nor should they have—that thirteen years later I would be married to (another) great love of my life and that we would have a messy, imperfect, and disarmingly beautiful life together. No one could have told me that I would find work that was deeply meaningful to me, a kind of work where I could keep her close to me always. No one could have told me that I would birth a child who in an instant would make my entire existence make sense—a child who would tether me to this world with roots so deep and unshakeable that, to this day, it takes my breath away. Even though I could not believe these events would come to pass, they did. In those early years following Diane's death, I could not imagine the life that was waiting for me. I could not imagine all of the possibilities that lay ahead, and this remains true for me today. While I know beyond a shadow of a doubt that more loss lies ahead—for me and for you—I am equally certain of the magic and possibility that will exist despite my current certainty of its unlikelihood. This is what I want you to fill your category one with. I want you to fill category one with all of the unlikely possibilities of your imagination.

In the fall of 2020, I turned forty. For a year prior to my fortieth birthday, I was knee-deep in planning a solo hike across northern Spain. All I wanted was to feel myself in space somewhere I'd never been. I wanted to really hear and experience myself apart from others. I wanted to test out this forty-year-old, post-kiddo body and see what surprises it had in store. For months, I meticulously planned out every detail; how many miles I would hike each day, which town I would end up in each evening. I chose the towns based on the restaurants I wanted to try. I spent hours looking up and translating their menus online, choosing what I wanted to eat at each place along the way. Researching the trip brought me an enormous amount of joy. Any spare minute I could find, I would jump onto my laptop and let myself fall into the bliss of planning. Obviously, in March of 2020, COVID-19 shut down the world, and I watched devastated as Spain, and so many other countries around the world, experienced catastrophic loss. I did not travel to Spain as initially planned. Instead, on my fortieth birthday, I found myself locked down in a small apartment in western Michigan with my wife, our kids, and our dog. Not exactly the solo adventure I had hoped for, but there we were, together and alive. When the world changed, so did my priorities. With the onset of the pandemic, suddenly being alone on a trip was inconsequential, and, instead, keeping my family safe became my sole priority. My wife is immunocompromised, so keeping our bubble protected and secure became our singular focus. I'm sharing this with you because not getting to go on this trip that I had so meticulously planned for taught me something. It taught me that not getting to go did nothing to diminish the profound joy I had experienced planning it. The glorious moments of falling into the rabbit hole of planning and researching had already happened. Nothing could take that away from me. In the end, not getting to go was almost irrelevant. Of course, I was disappointed, but by the time I was due to go, the world had changed, and so had I. Who knows if I will ever get myself to Spain; I am a different person than the person who began planning that trip all those years ago. COVID-19 has changed me; it has changed us all. Now almost four years later, I am knee-deep in the planning of a new trip. I am headed to Morocco with my daughter to introduce her to the sights and sounds (and mouth-watering tastes) of her people. Who knows? Maybe this time we will get there. All we can do is plan; the rest remains a mere possibility of our imagination.

There are two fundamental truths in this world: There is suffering, and there is not *only* suffering. Both are true. Full stop. One need not diminish the other's validity, and we need not use one to deny the reality of the other. When we are in the presence of suffering, we can be in it fully. No need to silver line the experience with toxic positivity. No need to move, hide, fade, or fix it. There is suffering. Similarly, when we are in the moments of life that are not suffering, moments of beauty, joy, birth, and excitement, we need not diminish those by reminding ourselves that suffering exists. A wise friend once told me, "Do not diminish your joy; hell is on its way." Ironically, the very thing that allows us to remain steadfast and solid in the presence of suffering is the amount of time we have spent not only suffering. Despite it seeming counterintuitive, the reason we get wobbly in the presence of suffering—whether it be our own or the suffering of others—and the reason we want to look away or offer an empty platitude to ease the discomfort is that when faced with the presence of true suffering, we are quick to forget that this is not the only truth. When in the presence of very real suffering, we find ourselves overwhelmed with the terror that this too could happen to us. We equally find ourselves overwhelmed with the idea that this may be our permanent reality. In the overwhelming panic, we begin to tell ourselves and others lies. We start our sentences with horrible phrases like "at least." We create stories of people being in better places, of things always happening for a reason, and of there being a greater purpose or plan at play. We unintentionally harm those we love most—and ourselves—by refusing to witness and honour the suffering exactly as it is. When we consciously and intentionally devote time to both imagination and possibility (category one), we start to create an internal reserve, a database of sorts, of the parts of life that are not only suffering. We create layers of narrative within ourselves rooted in experiences of delight, amusement, pleasure, and adventure. We remind ourselves over and over again that the ending is not yet known. When our internal reserves of imagination and possibility are full, we can pull from those reserves in times of suffering to help keep us solid and steady. When our cells and bones are brimming with the felt experiences of not only suffering, they do not feel the same need to collapse or recoil when suffering is present. Consider the time you spend filling up your category one as an insurance policy for the inevitable suffering that is to come.

When we spend too much time in the waters of grief and loss, and not enough time delighting from the shore, we start to cramp, and we begin to go under. A warning sign that you are spending too much time in the waters of grief and loss is the inability to access imagination and possibility. A lack of access to imagination and possibility is one of the most common indicators that it is time to come ashore, catch your breath, and dry off. It doesn't mean you cannot go back in. It doesn't mean your time in the ocean is complete. It simply means it is okay to take a minute, rest your body, and shift your gaze to the horizon.

Category Two: Maintenance

There are going to be times in our lives when, despite our best efforts, the water gets choppy. Sometimes, at no fault of our own, we are the recipient of our colleague's bad mood. Our kids get the stomach flu just as our aging parent has a fall. Our landlord informs us they are selling our apartment just as the car starts to make a concerning sound. Life is hard, and sometimes it can feel like a particular season is coming right for us, fists blazing. Despite having a well-maintained, solidly inflated flotation device, the waters are simply choppy, and you find yourself swallowing some serious saltwater. The water splashes you in the face, and it can feel like you barely catch your breath before another swell hits. These are the times we want to reach for category two, which is how we repair the natural, inevitable wear and tear of being human. Category two includes the activities you reach for at the end of a long week to restore the air that life has sucked out. They are activities requiring little time or resources to access but can replenish and restore your flotation device so that you are ready to get back out into the water safely. Often when I am explaining category two, someone will say, "I notice that some of my activities could be placed in both category two and three. How do I know where to put them?" Excellent question. I like to explain this answer by saying that category two is the long-weekend version of the activity in question. For example, cooking might be an activity that could technically be placed in either category two or three.

However, there is a difference between the kind of cooking that would occur in these two categories. Anyone can throw a pot of water on the stove and make boxed macaroni and cheese while screaming at their kid to get changed for their basketball practice that starts in twenty minutes. (This example may or may not be from personal lived experience.) Technically, this is cooking. However, it is a different experience from waking up leisurely on a Saturday morning and walking over to your local farmer's market. Perhaps you stroll through the market casually picking out fresh, seasonal produce. When you get home, you make yourself a cup of your favourite steeped tea while listening to music as you slowly prep your produce and begin making a delicious soup from your favourite cookbook. This is the kind of cooking I'm referring to in category two. Nothing hurried, nothing rushed. Slow, pleasurable, long-weekend versions of whatever the activity is. Enjoy.

Category Three: Crisis Management

I like to call category three crisis management. In times of crisis or conflict, we often have two choices available to us. We can make choices that will cause the crisis or conflict to escalate, or we can make choices that will interrupt its trajectory and therefore deescalate it. Often this can be the difference between pouring water on a fire vs. gasoline. If we want to learn how to stay afloat, we best learn how to reach for the water. There are going to be many, many moments in our lives where our nervous systems get activated. There are plenty of reasons for feeling enraged, overwhelmed, hopeless, and desperate. There are many prudent reasons to say, "Screw this!" while launching our flotation devices into the ocean. It may also serve us to learn how to step outside our flotation device, gently place it aside, and go for a walk to cool off before deciding if we want to shred it permanently. Category three is for those times when the waves blindside us and launch us from our floaties—the times when we are spit out like seaweed against the shore. In these moments, instead of responding to your boss in a heated fury or pushing it down and heading into your next session with a client, I want you to pause, breathe, and reach for category three. I want you to interrupt the escalation and acknowledge that you've been thrown into the sea. I want you to pause and recognize that you've been hurt and take a moment to assess the damage. I want you to reach for the water and not the gasoline. While you may not be able to repair the damage (that is what will occur when you have time to access category two), you can reach for category three to stop the bleeding and bandage the wound. There is very little in this life that cannot wait five minutes. You are worthy of the time it will take to reach for something from category three in order to witness and honour your own experience. This work is not just about filling our flotation devices so we stay afloat in other people's waters; it is about learning how to stay afloat in order to honour and navigate our own.

As we determined previously, if you are going to go swimming, you are going to get wet. You will never be able to predict or control the tides; you do not get a say in whether the waters are stormy or smooth. There will be days when you lazily float atop your floatie and take in the sun's rays. There will be days when the waves hit you head-on, and you swallow a significant amount of seawater. There will be times when the ocean flings you into its waters as quickly as it spits you back out, mouthfuls of salt and sand in tow. All you can do is make sure you are entering the waters with a flotation device that is as well maintained and inflated as possible. I truly believe that if you spend dedicated, intentional time filling up all three of these categories and use them accordingly, despite the occasional swell to the face, it is possible to stay afloat. Please do so. We need you.

For all of those in the dark and the dying.
May you be honored.
May your name be held holy.
May your body know comfort.
May a flicker of this love somehow find you,
and may you know yourself as held, here, in the light.

—Vigil, Isabel Abbott

Chapter Seven

Silenced

An Exploration of Mourning and Disenfranchised Grief

In chapter one, I defined mourning as what humans do with their involuntary grief responses to metabolize the inevitable losses accrued across the lifespan. When humans can mourn in the ways that work best for them, grief shifts from an unbearable individual burden to one whose weight is upheld by the collective. The reason for this is that it takes a community for one to mourn effectively. In chapter three, we discussed how community, storytelling, movement, and sound support the metabolization of grief. Although I firmly believe that mourning is something that every human being should have equitable access to, sadly, that is not the case. Mourning does not, and will not, happen on its own. In opposition to the involuntary nature of grief, there are four essential elements to mourning: time, space, capacity, and resources.

Time

As per Statistics Canada, as of 2022, 81.8 per cent of Canadian workers worked full-time (thirty or more hours per week). On top of the hours spent doing paid labour, women in particular spend an enormous amount of time doing unpaid labour. In 2019, a study found that Canadian women put in 820 hours of unpaid housework annually (Labbé). That same year, Statistics Canada found women with children averaged a little over fifteen hours a week of household labour, whereas men averaged just over ten, with women between twenty-five and fifty-four taking on the largest share of unpaid housework. Women in Ontario, who were found to do the highest share of housework, averaged 61.3 per cent of unpaid household labour. If time is money, then finding time to mourn, amid all of our paid and unpaid responsibilities, is very, very expensive.

With the exception of Nunavut, all provinces and territories have employment legislation policies that include some version of a bereavement leave policy (Wolfe). However, having a bereavement leave policy and having a bereavement leave policy responsive to the needs of bereaved people are two very different things. Canada's provincial bereavement leave policies range from one to ten days for the death of an immediate family member with three paid bereavement days being the most prevalent offering. Some of these policies offer paid time off; however, by and large, the vast majority of these policies are unpaid. In Ontario, Quebec, and the Yukon, employees are entitled to 104 unpaid days for the death of one's child. Even employers who offer three paid bereavement days do so only after three months of consecutive employment. Employers have full liberty to expand their current policies to better meet the needs of the bereaved. It is not the freedom that is lacking; it is the will to do so.

According to the Grief Institute's 2017 Grief Index, the death of an employee's loved one costs employers USD 49.3 billion in lost productivity (Zaslow). That number drops to USD 9.2 billion in the cases of losing extended family members, friends, and colleagues, while the death of a pet comes in around USD 3.1 billion. Having employees return to work prematurely following a loss is not just harmful to the employee; the numbers suggest it is bad for business as well. In the 2020 Society for Human Resource Management (SHRM) Employee Benefits Survey, almost all of the people who responded said that they took additional time off, including sick days, vacation time, or an extended leave of absence following their initial three days of bereavement leave. A 2021 report compiled by the Marie Curie charity found that 43 per cent of employees felt pressure to return to work before they were ready. John, a member of the Coalition of Bereaved Workers—a group coordinated by the Northern Ireland chapter of Marie Curie—said the following in his organization's call to action:

> I was given one day of paid time leave off when my [relative] died. One day was not enough and I was told I would have to take an unpaid day to attend the funeral. It made me feel like the company did not care about the wellbeing of their staff and that entire year I felt burnt out due to a lack of proper time off and rest. This was a major contributing factor to me finding alternative employment. (8)

The National Council for Palliative Care (NCPC) in the UK released a report in 2014 titled Life after Death: Six Steps to Improve Support in Bereavement. The report concluded that 58 per cent of employees felt their performance at work was affected by grief months after the death of a loved one. The report continues:

> [A] third of people [surveyed] (32 percent) said that they did not feel as though their employer treated them with compassion. ... The research found considerable public backing for bereavement support in the workplace, with more than four in five people (87 percent) agreeing all employers should have a compassionate employment policy, including paid bereavement leave, flexible working, and a range of other support. (NCPC)

Many bereaved people leave their jobs permanently within a year of experiencing a significant loss. I often share with HR professionals that the reason bereaved people leave their positions is not necessarily because anyone did anything wrong but is rather the result of no one having done anything right. When your assumptive world has been shattered, it can be an incredibly painful experience to return to a job where nothing externally reflects the magnitude of the shift a bereaved person has experienced internally. The bereaved person might look the same from the outside, but their entire world has changed, so when colleagues quickly return to the status quo it can often feel like their reality is being erased. The bereaved can often feel as though their reality—their pain and loss—is invisible to those around them. Bereaved people don't necessarily leave their positions for a better job or a higher salary; often they leave to inhabit a work environment that is as foreign to them externally as they experience themselves internally, therefore offering them an experience of psychological congruence.

IN PRACTICE

Here are what some bereavement leave advocates around the globe are saying:

Eve Richardson, Chief Executive of the National Council for Palliative Care and the Dying Matters Coalition, commented:

> The costs of bereavement are too great to ignore, both for individuals and for society. Employers have an important role to play by being compassionate and having a bereavement policy in place. They should also ensure that they support their managers so that they are confident in having sensitive discussions about end-of-life issues with their staff. It is also often the little things that matter and help make a difference, such as kind words from a manager or a card to say we are thinking of you. With the number of people dying each year set to increase there's never been a more important time to get bereavement support right, both in the workplace and throughout society. (NCPC)

Dawn Chaplin, cofounder of the National Bereavement Alliance, said:

> Learning to live with the loss of someone close is one of the most painful experiences we can encounter, and society's response often makes it even harder. There's an urgent need to improve access to bereavement services, and to ensure that people who have been bereaved are not ignored or left isolated. (NCPC)

Lucy Herd, founder of Jack's Rainbow, who has been campaigning for the British government to review statutory bereavement leave since the death of her young son Jack in August 2010, added:

> Much more must be done to provide support to people who have been bereaved. It's completely unrealistic to expect people who have lost someone close to them to immediately go back to work and carry on as normal. That's why we need a new approach to how we support people who have been bereaved, so that they get the support they need whenever they need it. (NCPC)

Mourning requires time, and not just a singular experience of time. Mourning requires more time than it takes to bury the dead, find a new home, immigrate, or land a new job. Mourning, like grief, will require our attention for as long as we are alive. Given how little employers offer in terms of paid bereavement leave, in addition to all of the other unpaid responsibilities we have, it is unsurprising that few of us have any real access to the time needed for mourning.

Space

Bereaved people need physical spaces to mourn. For some, this might be space in the privacy of their own home, whereas for others it might be access to nature and the outdoors. We need physical spaces to provide us with the container in which mourning can occur. For some bereaved people, the need might be for the physical space to provide a sense of safety and containment (e.g., the security of one's bedroom). For others, the preferred space for mourning might embody a sense of vastness (shorelines, forests, mountains, etc.). For years after Diane died, I sought out geographical locations that made me feel small and insignificant in comparison. I could only tolerate the enormity of my grief when I was in an environment that was expansive enough to hold it. It was in these environments that I could finally breathe. Amid the vastness, there was enough space for my grief to exist without swallowing and suffocating me whole. In these surroundings, I could experience myself as more than my grief. It was where I could see myself as a teeny tiny, somewhat unimportant piece of a much larger whole; a space where her death wasn't personal or punitive, but rather the inevitable outcome of every single living creature that has ever existed. The experiences I have in these types of spaces are best expressed by British biologist Richard Dawkins:

> We are going to die, and that makes us the lucky ones. Most people are never going to die because they are never going to be born. The potential people who could have been here in my place but who will in fact never see the light of day outnumber the sand grains of Arabia. Certainly, those unborn ghosts include greater poets than Keats, scientists greater than Newton. We know this because the set of possible people allowed by our DNA so massively exceeds the set

> of actual people. In the teeth of these stupefying odds, it is you and I, in our ordinariness, that are here. We privileged few, who won the lottery of birth against all odds, how dare we whine at our inevitable return to that prior state from which the vast majority have never stirred? (1)

Physical spaces offer powerful containers for mourning. The bereaved need to have access to spaces to mourn in the ways that feel safest and best for them. An ideal space for one person might be the complete opposite for another. What feels right in year one following a loss might be entirely different from what feels right in year two. There is no right or wrong space in which to mourn. Over the years, many people have shared with me their favourite spaces to mourn, including the shower, their car, in the bathtub, at live concerts, on pilgrimages, while camping, on an airplane, and countless more. Find the space that allows you to breathe—where you and your grief can both live free.

Capacity (Aka "Spoons")

In her 2003 essay "The Spoon Theory," Christine Miserandino writes about living with lupus and her attempts at explaining it to a friend. While at a restaurant, Christine grabbed a number of spoons off the table and handed them to her friend. The number of spoons represented how much energy she had to spend throughout the day. She used the spoons to demonstrate that people with chronic illness often begin their days with limited quantities of energy—or spoons—compared to their non-chronically ill peers. She asked her friend to list off all the things she does in a day (get up, brush her teeth, shower, take the subway to work, etc.). As her friend listed off the different tasks she completed throughout her day, Christine took away one spoon for each activity. The exercise illustrated how people with chronic illness have to plan their lives and activities around the limited number of spoons they have each day. Spoon theory is also frequently used to describe the lived experience of those with invisible disabilities. People with invisible disabilities often display no obvious, visible indicators of their disability and, as such, are often perceived as lazy, unreliable, or deceitful by those who have no lived experience of chronic illness or disability. The premise of spoon theory can be similarly applied to the bereaved. While grief is not a disability, the impacts of it can absolutely be disabling. When people are grieving, the number of spoons they have to get through each day is limited at best. Mourning uses and requires a significant number of spoons, and this is where the bereaved require their community to step in and share the load. For a bereaved person to allocate any of their very limited and precious spoons to mourning, there needs to be others who generously, and regularly, offer their energy and capacity to help increase the pool of spoons available. Following a loss, the community is not needed solely for emotional support or a listening ear; the community is often needed to take on the brunt of the unpaid, invisible labour (e.g., cooking, cleaning, and childcare) so that the bereaved person can access the energy—or spoons—required for mourning.

Resources

The costs of mourning in our culture are astronomical. I mentioned earlier how employees are not offered any substantial paid time off, making the time and resources needed to mourn entirely inaccessible. Additionally, the spaces people need to mourn can be equally inaccessible due to financial costs. With the average cost of a home in Canada reaching $735, 900 in April of 2024, millions of Canadians cannot afford basic housing, let alone access to their preferred spaces for mourning (Solomon). For those living in a city, accessing nature often requires money for transportation. When we look at the immediate need for rituals of mourning following a death, the average cost of a traditional funeral with burial in Canada is currently between $5,000 and $10,000 (Levy-Ward). An Angus Reid poll conducted in May 2023 reveals that a majority of Canadians would face challenges in affording funeral expenses when a loved one dies (Walker). The study also found that 78 per cent of respondents would feel financially vulnerable due to funeral-related expenses. Due to the enormous financial costs associated with traditional funerals, it is no wonder why so many Canadians are opting out of them altogether. According to 2021 data from the Cremation Association of North America, 74.8 per cent of deaths in Canada now result in cremation (Owen). Unfortunately, when people decide to forgo a traditional funeral, they often unintentionally forgo the opportunity to mobilize support from their communities. Christy Denckla is a research associate at the Harvard TH Chan School of Public Health and a clinical psychologist specializing in grief. Here she shares her thoughts on the importance of funerals and rituals of mourning:

> Funerals and the rituals that go along with mourning that loss are really fundamental to a number of processes. They're fundamental to how we mourn, to how we grieve, to how we reinforce social ties, to how we expand the social safety net in times of vulnerability and loss. And more fundamentally, they reflect what it means for us to be human and for us to love and for us to connect. (qtd. in Doubek and Doubek)

What are we losing when our traditional ways of mourning become inaccessible to us? How are these financial barriers impeding our ability to metabolize our grief? When we forgo traditional funerals and rituals of mourning, and instead host celebrations of life often months after a death has occurred, I worry that we are simply increasing our culture's aversion to loss and replacing the experience with a distanced, sanitized version of mourning that avoids the hard and often painful work of metabolizing grief.

Despite knowing that an ongoing combination of community, storytelling, movement, and sound supports the metabolization of grief, due to the violent nature of capitalism, these things remain widely inaccessible for most people due to the financial costs involved. Any of the somatic or body-based therapies and practices (e.g., massage, acupuncture, osteopathy, etc.) that may help attend to the physical impacts of grief are expensive and often require repeat visits to experience any meaningful, long-term benefits. For those who find having the individual support of a therapist beneficial, the average cost for a single session is between $150 and $250 an hour. For those who need time off of work to be with their community, to tend to grieving children, and to acclimate to the shattering of their assumptive world, there are very few options to do so without significant financial repercussions, particularly for low-income earners. When financial barriers prevent us from being able to access the things we need to mourn effectively, we end up with millions of people who are living with alarming amounts of unmetabolized, obstructed grief.

Given that most of us were not able to access these key elements of mourning following the COVID-19 pandemic, it is not surprising to me in the slightest that four years later, we are seeing increased levels of violence, division, and the widespread deterioration of social and societal contracts. How could it be otherwise? If the purpose of mourning is to support the metabolization of grief so that we have space and capacity for additional attachments, then the opposite is also true. An inability to mourn effectively will decrease and impede our capacity for attachment. With devastating effects, we are currently witnessing the ways these barriers to attachment are taking us further and further away from what makes us most human. Our lack of access to these four key elements of mourning is making us behave in ways that are more and more inhumane.

Disenfranchised Grief

The term "disenfranchised grief" was coined by Dr. Kenneth J. Doka in 1989 and refers to "the grief that persons experience when they incur a loss that is not or cannot be openly acknowledged, publicly mourned, or socially supported" (4). Doka goes on to explain that disenfranchised grief commonly occurs in the following circumstances:

1. **When the loss is not recognized**. The mourner's social world, society at large, or both do not acknowledge the loss. Examples include perinatal deaths, miscarriages, losses associated with abortion and adoption, and invisible losses such as those associated with dementia, Alzheimer's, chronic illness, and disability. These losses are often dismissed or minimized by those around the bereaved; consequently, the loss is not publicly mourned or socially supported.
2. **When the relationship is not socially sanctioned or acknowledged as being significant**. Examples include the loss of extramarital partners, nonbiological, chosen family members, teachers, mentors, ex-spouses or former in-laws, pets, and service animals, etc. In theory, these relationships may be recognized as relationships, but they are not recognized as relationships that would be worthy of mourning and bereavement, therefore decreasing the likelihood that the loss will be acknowledged openly or that the mourner will be offered the appropriate social support.
3. **When the circumstances of the loss are stigmatized**. Examples include losses due to suicide, addiction, criminal activity and/or poverty. The circumstances of the loss and the stigma that

accompanies it impede the mourner from accessing social support or publicly mourning their loss.

4. **When the bereaved person is not recognized as being able to grieve and is therefore not acknowledged as someone in need of mourning.** Examples include young children, the elderly, those with developmental and/or intellectual disabilities, and those with cognitive impairments. If someone is not granted the role of mourner, they are often excluded from mourning rituals and are not offered the same opportunity to mourn publicly, nor are they likely to be offered social support from others.
5. **When the bereaved person's grief responses and/or chosen ways of mourning are deemed socially inappropriate.** Rituals of mourning are entirely dependent on culture, so what is appropriate in one culture might be wildly inappropriate in another. When someone's grief style or way of mourning is incongruent with social and societal norms, it makes others around them uncomfortable. They will therefore likely experience social rejection and isolation as a result. This makes the possibility of accessing social support both difficult and unlikely.

When we consider the ways humans metabolize grief, along with the key elements required for mourning, it is easy to see how those who experience disenfranchised grief are greatly disadvantaged. If a loss is not or cannot be openly acknowledged, publicly mourned, or socially supported, there is little likelihood that grief will be metabolized well. When we look at communities whose grief has been historically disenfranchised (e.g., Indigenous, Black, racialized, 2SLGBTQIA+, disabled, and spoonie communities), it is easy to see the correlation between their disproportionately poor health outcomes and their long histories of disenfranchised grief.

The Cultural Appropriation of Grief Rites and Rituals

The *Cambridge Dictionary* defines cultural appropriation as "the act of taking or using things from a culture that is not your own, especially without showing that you understand or respect this culture." *Wikipedia* defines it as "the inappropriate or unacknowledged adoption of an element or elements of one culture or identity by members of another culture or identity." Cultural appropriation is particularly problematic when those who are appropriating hold more power and privilege than the culture and communities from which they are taking. Cultural appropriation can include the exploitation of another culture's religious and cultural traditions, dance steps, fashion, symbols, language, and music (Rogers). As they are removed from their cultural contexts, important elements are lost or distorted during the appropriation. The appropriated element is then often used in ways that demonstrate a lack of respect and reverence for the culture and people to whom it originally belonged. Cultural elements that may have deep meaning to the originating culture may be reduced to exotic fashion or toys by those from the dominant culture (Houska). Kjerstin Johnson has written that when this is done, the imitator, "who does not experience that oppression, is able to 'play,' temporarily, an 'exotic' other, without experiencing any of the daily discriminations faced by other cultures."

You might be wondering: What does this have to do with grief and loss? Given that our culture has all but erased any form of grief literacy from our institutions of higher learning, our educational curriculums, and public discourse, we are left with a culture bereft of commonly shared mourning rituals. As previously discussed, even those of us who individually come from cultures with long histories of beautiful, rich mourning practices are often not able to access them due to the ongoing impacts of colonialism and capitalism. In the absence of shared mourning rituals, many settlers in Canada and the United States have culturally appropriated grief rites and rituals from other cultures. This becomes particularly problematic when the mourning rituals of a historically oppressed culture (e.g., Indigenous peoples in Canada) are taken out of context by those (settlers) who have historically oppressed them and who lack the cultural context to understand, respect, or lead these rituals. Many First Nations people in Australia have spoken out against the cultural appropriation of their sweat lodge and vision quest ceremonies by settlers and even by tribes who have not traditionally had these ceremonies. They contend that there are serious safety risks whenever these events are conducted by those who lack the many years of training and cultural immersion required to lead them safely (Byard and Riches). We previously established that when grief cannot be openly acknowledged, publicly mourned, or socially supported, it will become disenfranchised and therefore is less likely to be metabolized, which can then lead to long-term adverse health outcomes. If members of a historically oppressed group cannot access their traditional ways of mourning while simultaneously having their lived experiences of loss systematically denied, their grief will be disenfranchised, and the likelihood of adverse health outcomes will follow. To have one's grief disenfranchised in this way, and then to witness the same people who caused this disenfranchisement appropriate the rituals of mourning you are no longer able to access, is an act of violence.

One of the methods I have developed for myself to ensure that I am not appropriating, and therefore behaving in ways that are misaligned with my values, is to consider what I call the three C's: consent, credit, and compensation.

1. Consent: Have I asked for consent from the people to whom this cultural element originally belongs? Have they said yes?
2. Credit: If they have consented, have I given credit and proper acknowledgement to those to whom this cultural element originally belongs?
3. Compensation: If they have consented and I have given due credit, have I appropriately compensated those to whom this cultural element originally belongs?

If the answer to any of the above is no, I urge you to reconsider your use of the cultural element you have taken. However unintentional, using the grief rites and rituals of cultures that are not your own, without the explicit consent from those to whom it belongs (in addition to offering the appropriate compensation), is unacceptable.

IN PRACTICE

In an online piece titled "Reclaiming Cultural Teachings about Mortality, Grief, Loss, Death, and Dying," Chrystal Waban Toop, a member of the Algonquins of Pikwakanagan First Nation, shared some of her insights on mortality, culture, and approaches to grief. Below is an excerpt from the article highlighting her thoughts on the cultural appropriation of Indigenous grief practices:

> Though I have been asked to share ceremonies here about end-of-life [EOL] and after death, this too requires a pause and measuring for potential harms. End-of-life spaces are fraught with cultural appropriation, and this is its own, on-going trauma. Consider the impacts on Indigenous people who do not carry their teachings as a direct result of systemic racism. Consider how a First Nation, Inuit, or Metis person would feel when a non-Indigenous person shares ceremonial practices and teachings that have been observed and appropriated for their own benefit. There are numerous benefits to non-Indigenous EOL practitioners who decide to offer Indigenous ceremonies in their practices of care, including but not limited to raising their own profiles as 'spiritual practitioners' and financial incentives.
>
> Just the other day one of the death care groups I belong to on social media promoted an event and training offered by a non-Indigenous EOL practitioner who not only offered an expensive practitioner training, but also authored several books on Indigenous practices, without an ounce of Indigenous identity. These individuals profit and make livings off teachings obtained in ceremonial spaces.
>
> When our cultural teachers provide teachings, there is a great responsibility in receiving and honouring these teachings on cultural practices. As a carrier of these teachings, we must always practice ethically, conscientious of the belief that teachings are not to be monetized while simultaneously balancing a very real need to take care of ourselves and our families.

Before you pay a non-Indigenous person to teach you Indigenous culture, please question what nation these teachings genuinely belong to and do the hard work of reflecting on whether you need this teaching for your practice and if you genuinely support Indigenous people. If the answer is no, I want to congratulate you on your very real efforts to decolonize your thinking and your EOL practice.

If your pursuit of these teachings eclipses the needs of those who are Indigenous and reclaiming what was taken, please check yourself and your privilege. I am often dumbfounded by the willingness of those who pay non-Indigenous practitioners for culture but refuse to practice diligence to ensure payment of actual Indigenous community members for the same, without ethical lines being crossed.

Chrystal is a proud Anishinaabekwe and a member of the rural Indigenous community of Renfrew County. She is a counselor and Indigenous death doula.

Human Stories of Disenfranchised Grief

Essays from the Margins

Disenfranchised Grief: A Love Story

Oh, how I loved him. This big, bold and beautiful man. Convinced by friends that we should meet, I opened my apartment door on our first date and that. was. it. On the second date, he told me he was both HIV and HEPC positive, coinfected by "tainted" blood given to thousands during the 1980s and 1990s. As a hemophiliac, he didn't stand a chance. Dependent on that borrowed blood for life, it now spelled his death. And yet, he was oh so alive, so clear of mind, heart and spirit. He would live this life, every tiny inch of it until the end, and I would live it with him for as long as we had. So, there were years of joy, adventure, laughter, long talks and the kind of love that makes you want to climb up on a roof and shout, "Do you see this magic over here?" And there was social silence and half-truths and always, a disenfranchised kind of anticipatory and then forever grief that haunts, hurts and hinders.

Early on in our love, I learned about the Krever Inquiry in Canada, about the class action suits for those who had been infected and the "blood money" being paid to survivors and families by the federal government. Early on, he told me why he had mostly kept his silence. He said that one of two things happened when he revealed his status. Either the person became acutely afraid and distanced, or the person became so worried about him that it would negatively impact their health and well-being. Exhibit A: The woman he had loved and who had left him. Exhibit B.

The parent who had died suddenly. So, along with the silencing legalities, I honoured his wishes, and no one knew except a very tiny circle of family and one trusted friend. That continued after his sudden, horrifying death, through all the mess of the legal and administrative kind, through the family fissures, anxiety and PTSD diagnoses, through the attempts by the government to "claw" back the blood money, through all the years of wanting it to be over.

But it's not quite over. I cannot write his name. I cannot say that my beloved was killed. His life was disenfranchised, the reasons for his death were too, as is my ongoing grief at the magnitude of this loss. But it is not all silence these days. Here I am, writing for us, and there are more kin who know now, with whom I can say more of the truth. And there is the knowing that as I am writing this, in the UK, survivors and families of the tainted blood scandal are just now getting the acknowledgement they have long fought for. I want to hope that the acknowledgement releases them from the state denial they have experienced. I want us all to feel that this is the kind of justice necessary for healing disenfranchised lives, death and grief. But deep in my bones, I am not sure. Not sure what kind of practice could ever really heal us, but writing this, knowing you are reading it, somehow is part of the process.

—Anonymous

The Commission of Inquiry on the Blood System in Canada, also known as the Krever Inquiry, was a public investigation of the Canadian blood system, which had been contaminated with the HIV and hepatitis C viruses during the 1980s. In 1993, a public inquiry into the Canadian blood system was established, and Justice Horace Krever was named commissioner. The infection of thousands of Canadians with (HIV) and hepatitis C is Canada's worst-ever preventable public health disaster. It has also become one of its most prolonged legal sagas, featuring a high-profile public inquiry, almost $10 billion in legal claims, and a criminal investigation. At least two thousand recipients of blood and blood products contracted HIV between 1980 and 1985. Another thirty thousand transfusion recipients were infected with hepatitis C, a potentially debilitating liver disease between 1980 and 1990. About 8,000 of those who received contaminated blood products are expected to die as a result (The Canadian Encyclopedia).

The Doctor Will *See* You Now

Kanyen'keha:ka wakhskaré:wake tehanakari:ne tsi niwaki'taro:ten. Similar to the way my brain functions, my storytelling goes down many pathways, branching off, exploring various nonlinear trains of thought. When I think of the ways in which grief has followed me throughout my life, I cannot locate a time when it wasn't present; and yet, it has been difficult for me to recognize it at times, especially since our society is not built to acknowledge grief but rather to pathologize it as a maladaptive behaviour. As someone who is continuously learning how to let the experience of grief flow through me, I am committed to the ongoing navigation of this complex landscape; I care for myself so that I can care for others. I am Mohawk, grew up on a reserve, and am the first in five generations of my family's lineage to not attend residential school. I am a Queer, neurodivergent woman living in a bigger body. These intersections shape my lived experience and amplify the grief that stems from both personal loss and continued cultural disruption.

I was swimming in the waters of grief, enveloped in the sorrow that marked my entry into the world just as my father departed it. My mom was six months pregnant with me when my dad died. Today, as I write this, it happens to be the anniversary of his death. Thirty-one years ago, he was killed in a car accident. He was only twenty-eight years old when he died. He had a fiancée, a one-year-old daughter, and another on the way (me). He was the baby of seventeen. His sudden death shook the whole family deeply. To this day, there are family members who cannot see me without crying. They continue to carry the weight of grief all these years later. I was born early just a few weeks after his death. My mom was told by our Elders that I arrived early to help ease her grief. It's possible that my arrival did help to ease her grief a little, however, coming out looking like him, and growing into someone who behaved very much like him, I also compounded it.

I have always had this sense inside myself that I was running out of time. There was always this deep seeded, unconscious belief that I was going to die young. I didn't know until much later in life that this is a common belief children often develop when they lose a parent young. As I grew, I had this insatiable drive to seek out every possible opportunity; to live my life to the fullest. I was even made fun of for this because I was always on the go, always doing so many different things. After completing multiple degrees, travelling to over fifty countries including all seven continents, I was inching towards twenty-eight and I found myself feeling overwhelmed. I soon realized I was almost the same age my dad was when he died. I hadn't realized I was trying to accomplish as much as I could before this particular milestone. It's hard to explain, but it felt like a looming deadline. And then, I turned twenty-eight; and I didn't die. I turned twenty-nine, and thirty, and experienced all these ages and years that my dad never got to live. I am not always aware of the ways in which his death and absence have impacted me. There are the obvious ways of course, like the pain of seeing fathers and daughters have tender moments in public, or never fully knowing him and which traits I have that are his. However, there are other more subtle ways too, like realizing that I have never envisioned my children having a father of their own.

I can't count the number of times people have told me that I have experienced more loss in the time they've known me than they have in their entire lives. While writing this, I started a list to see if I had a rough number of the people I have lost. Conservatively, I listed seventy-three people off the top of my head. Friends and family who have died by suicide, those who have died from preventable health issues, and those who died suddenly in accidents like my dad. Only a small number have died older, and the vast majority were sudden and unexpected. This keeps me in a constant state of mourning. There isn't a single month where I am not aware of the dates that pass by. As time moves forward all of these life events cluster together. My best friend had her second baby; my grandma died on New Year's Eve; my friend died on New Year's Day; the day following my uncle died, and another uncle again a few days after that; a dear friend died by suicide on one of our friends' birthdays, which was just days before her own birthday. It just keeps going and going, a repetitive cycle of birth days and death days. Each one a landmark in a sea of memories of those I love and those I have lost.

When I think of all that my people have lost, have had stolen from them, I am immediately overcome with love for our stubbornness—it is how we have survived. We have held on tightly to anything and everything we could because there is no aspect of our culture that has not been altered by settlers and colonization. Trying to get non-Indigenous people to understand this has been its own experience of disenfranchisement. Take for instance the calendar that marks the holidays we acknowledge. They all centre around Christianity, around the religion of those who colonized Turtle Island. We live by this rigid seven-day week where the days of rest align with Abrahamic religions. The only holidays my people have off are the holidays of those who colonized them. When someone dies, we are offered three days of bereavement leave because this is the amount of time that settlers' traditions and timelines allow for. We aren't even asked what our traditions are, or how much time we need for our ceremonies of Condolence. It is meant to be a process of holding our grief collectively, spread out across our family, our Clan, and our Nation. This process takes time; time that many aren't granted. Not only has this ceremony been disrupted, but key aspects of our culture as a whole have been lost including many of our traditions around death, dying, grief and loss. It is impossible to measure all that has been taken from the ongoing efforts to systematically erase our culture, our language, and our people. In my culture, when someone dies, we all have responsibilities to the families within our clan. Many people no longer know who their clan family is, and as such, our responsibility to the other families within our clan is interrupted or not able to be honoured. This results in some families being alone in their time of grief, scrambling to make funeral arrangements, cook food, etc. The other families in their clan don't know it is their duty to take over, yet they can't be blamed for not fulfilling their duties of stepping in and completing these tasks, of holding space and caring for them, when all this knowledge has been lost, taken. We aren't supposed to grieve like this; grieving is a ceremony, a space for the collective, to care and be cared for. We cannot do this in three days; no one can, and no one should. We have been removed from this sacred process. We have been forcibly removed from so much; from nature, from the land we care for, from the very clay we are made of. There are barriers that still exist today preventing our access to the natural world and to the cycle of these ceremonies. And yet, we are a stubborn people, and against all odds we continue to honour our own ways of knowing and being.

Indigenous people continue to be ignored and excluded from public narratives. We watch as popular media moves towards more diverse representation and yet Indigenous representation continues to be largely absent. Reserves aren't featured on maps, nor on road information signs as destinations. Our children are overrepresented within the child welfare system. Our people are incarcerated at disproportionate rates. The willful ignorance of settlers regarding our lack of access to housing, food, education, jobs, and even modern necessities like Wi-Fi, all adds to our experiences of erasure. The settler communities around my reserve all have clean drinking water and yet our home, in 2024, still does not. My entire life I have watched as settlers live on our land and benefit from the dispossession and oppression of our people. They continue to read their statements acknowledging the theft of our land, the genocide of our people, with absolutely no movement to return the land, or to reallocate the profits they continue to make from it. They do not see us in the present, only willing to acknowledge the past. All of these are painful examples of how the grief of my people is not openly acknowledged, publicly mourned or socially supported. This is the lived experience of disenfranchised grief.

English cannot capture our experience; settlers will never understand the weight of belonging to the land, to a Clan, a Nation. We do and always will. I will always know the clay I am made of and the people I am responsible to.

Kanyen'keha:ka wakhskaré:wake tehanakari:ne tsi niwaki'taro:ten.

—Dr. Yotakahron Jonathan

Dr. Yotakahron Jonathan, is a Mohawk Bear clan from Six Nations of the Grand River, where she was born and raised. She is an auntie, a doula, and is currently completing her medical residency on many First Nations' territories through the University of British Columbia's Indigenous Family Medicine program.

I would cross the bridges,
all of them
again and again,
every time, in every life,
to walk with you in this world.

—remember, Isabel Abbott

Epilogue

While the beginning of this book dawned along the edge of the Atlantic Ocean, it was completed deep in the wilderness of a Western Michigan forest. In the early years after Diane died, I was consumed with wanting to write our story. The story of her and I. I wanted to share her with the whole world. I was desperate for the world to know the magnitude of what it had lost. I wanted her legacy to be solidified and sustained. For many reasons, some known and others unknown, that story did not arise. Instead, the story of her and I has evolved into the single most private truth I carry. I hold it as close to my chest as my own heart still beating. All these years later, she and I exist in a space beyond language. She exists in the space where music lives, and in the space where ocean, wilderness, and horizon all meet—in the faint, forever elusive line between here and there. She exists in spaces that can be inhabited and felt but not spoken. For it is in the very act of speaking that she is once again lost.

Today, as I made my way through the winding trails of the forest, something startling yet so completely obvious occurred to me. The story of her and I is not one she would want told. Di was one of the most private people I have ever met. She kept her inner workings quiet and hidden. Her persona was larger than life, but her fears and truths were not for public consumption. At her core, Di was an educator not a performer. Performing wasn't what brought her the most joy; teaching others and being a part of someone else's growth was what lit her up from the inside. She was obsessed with unpacking lyrics and music to help her students get to the core of a piece—to discover something true within themselves, something human. When she was just weeks away from death, I asked her what she wanted to do with the time she had left. Without a moment's hesitation, she said,

"I want to teach again." I messaged her students and in less than twenty-four hours, we all gathered in the chapel of an emptied church on a weekday afternoon, and one by one, we stood to sing one final time for the woman we so loved.

Six days before she died, we were in the car driving to a medical appointment when she unfolded a piece of paper to show me a sketch she had done. She told me that it was the logo for the company she wanted to launch once she got better. She said being sick had made it clear to her that she wanted to go into musical direction and arrangement full-time. She didn't want to perform or audition anymore. She wanted instead to be the conduit between the music and the performer—the one who took something good and turned it into magic. Of course, more than having her own story told, Di would want the wisdom that her life and death inspired to be shared. She would want her life and death to serve as an opportunity for growth and new learning in the world.

Di once told me that I was a tall poppy. She said it was risky being a tall poppy because plants are expected to grow at the same speed and height. Those that grow too tall are often cut down and diminished. What I know with absolute certainty is that if I am in any way a tall poppy, it is only because she is the soil in which I grew. And perhaps that is why it took eighteen years for this story—the right story—to arise because learning and growth cannot be rushed. They take time, patience, nurturing, and fortitude. They require both sun and rain and the wisdom of years gone by.

Acknowledgments

A random, often unknown, fact about me is that I have three dates tattooed on the back of my neck. Because I have long hair, the tattoo is not easily visible. Those who have seen it often assume that the dates mark important or special occasions, and although that is not incorrect, it is also incomplete. The dates on my neck are the dates of days that changed everything. Dates that changed me. The dates aren't about good or bad moments, special or celebratory. They are the dates that mark a moment of before and a moment of after. Dates that once they'd occurred meant I would never again go back to who I was prior. Many beautiful and painful experiences have impacted me in my life. Moments of celebration and accomplishment, moments of heartache and disappointment. All of these moments matter; however, it is not true that they all fundamentally changed the core of who I am. Three dates—and three people—have changed me irrevocably, and I would like to begin with them.

The first date on my tattoo is the day Diane died. Although that day forever changed my life, it would perhaps be more accurate to rewind the clock and list the date of her birth as the one that matters most. While her death—and all that came after—remains the impetus for this book, it is her life that mattered to me most. It is that vibrant, direct, fearless, and wildly talented human I would like to acknowledge and thank here. Yes, her death forever changed my experience of being human but so did her love. Watching her parent made me choose to become one myself. Caring for her showed me that I would be capable of doing so when the time came. I will never know why she chose me or why of all the people it was me who she let in close, but I am so, *so* eternally grateful she did. Di, loving you was, and remains, the easiest thing I have ever done. Thank you. For all of it. For everything, every moment. For you.

The second date is the day my baby came into the world. Kesem, you made me a mama, and in doing so, you are my wildest dream come true. Thank you for always speaking truth, for always making me laugh until my belly hurts, and for reminding me how perfectly and exquisitely magical we all are. You have the bravest and most willing heart I have ever encountered. Thank you for coming and thank you for being mine. You are my whole heart, Goose. Never forget how much I love you or lose sight of the profound joy your existence has brought to mine, even after I am gone—especially after I am gone.

The final date is the day I met my wife. I'm not sure what there is left to say that has not already been said, but Isabel, you must know that you are what has made everything and anything that came before worthwhile. Your love and support are unwavering. Thank you for always being on my side, for always amusing and delighting me. Thank you for the petty and the irreverent, the laughter and the vanity, the steadfastness and the sure. You are my favourite human being and my very best friend. I long for decades and decades of you, of us, together. May we grow so very old and always find our way home. From the bottom of my heart, thank you.

The island. The place that held me as the words came, as eighteen years of labour and grief were put to the page. A place of exposed, raw beauty, a place where heat, ocean, and horizon all merge. To the places that allowed me to sit and write for hours on end: Café Mogagua, oh my brunch! and Café Bambu. To my dear friend Sandra Herrera, thank you for your friendship and hospitality. Thank you for the avocado toast and eggs, the smoothies, and cinnamon rolls. For always making sure I was fed and fuelled and for trusting me with your gorgeous, grieving heart. Muchas gracias, amiga.

It takes so very much for a single book to come into existence. It too requires time, space, capacity, and resources. It requires others doing school pickups and basketball practice drop-offs and for kids to be willing to eat eggs for dinner for days and weeks on end. It requires people and friends who show up endlessly in extraordinary and mundane ways. It requires all of those who came before, those who taught and inspired, those who led by example, and those who showed different ways of being and doing. It requires physical places and spaces to hold all that is being birthed. I could not have done this alone; I *have* not done this alone. This book is a culmination of the efforts and support—the stories and lives—of so many people and so many places. I hope to have done them justice.

Works Cited

Abbott, Isabel. *Salt + Honey*. Self-Published, 2016. https://www.amazon.ca/Salt-Honey-secular-prayers-hedonistic/dp/ 0692723439/ref=sr_1_1?crid=3498ZPG12HBF6&dib=eyJ2IjoiMSJ9.2TaYR2n_0z6SvmbIjBDxD7BASokVkbbVnSOhC-gJZmt8SjhWNrlvlR7wpXiR5qP9EPU_t4Tt-nwhFVZzkDDLf2A&dib_tag=se&keywords=salt+ and+honey+isabel+abb. Accessed 17 June 2024.

Animal Care and Use Office. *Social Species*, https://az.research.umich.edu/animalcare/glossary/social-species#:~:text=Species%20regarded%20as%20highly%20 interactive,rabbits%2C%20sheep%2C%20and%20swine. Accessed 17 June 2024.

"Audre Lorde." *Poetry Foundation*, 2017. https://www.poetryfoundation.org/poets/audre-lorde. Accessed 17 June 2024.

Ben-Joseph, Elana P. "Sleep and Your 1-to-2-Year-Old." *KidsHealth*, 2019, https://kidshealth.org/en/parents/sleep12yr.html. Accessed 17 June 2024.

Berns, Nancy. "Beyond Closure: Nancy Berns at TEDxDesMoines." *YouTube*, uploaded by TEDx Talks, 2012, https://www.youtube.com/watch?v=w0rCfXSdYPE&ab_channel=TEDxTalks. Accessed 17 June 2024.

Berns, Nancy. "Closure: The Rush to End Grief and What It Costs Us." Temple University Press, 2011.

Bogin, Barry. "The Evolution of Human Growth." *Human Growth and Development*. Edited by Barry Bogin. Academic Press, 2013, pp. 285–293.

Bonanno, G. *The Other Side of Sadness: What the New Science of Bereavement Tells Us about Life After Loss*. Basic Books, 2009.

Bradbeer, Mark, et al. "Widowhood and Other Demographic Associations of Pain in Independent Older People." *The Clinical Journal of Pain*, vol. 19, no. 4, 2003, pp. 247–54. *PubMed*, https://doi.org/10.1097/00002508-200307000-00008.

Branigin, Anne. "Women Are 32% More Likely to Die Post-Op If Their Surgeon Is a Man, Study Finds." *The Lily*, 2022. https://www.thelily.com/women-are-32-more-likely-to-die-post-op-if-their-surgeon-is-a-man-study-finds/. Accessed 17 June 2024.

Buckley, Thomas, et al. "Physiological Correlates of Bereavement and the Impact of Bereavement Interventions." *Dialogues in Clinical Neuroscience*, vol. 14, no. 2, June 2012, pp. 129–39.

Byard, Roger W., and Karen J. Riches. "Dehydration and Heat-Related Death: Sweat Lodge Syndrome." *The American Journal of Forensic Medicine and Pathology*, vol. 26, no. 3, Sept. 2005, p. 236. *journals.lww.com*, https://doi.org/10.1097/01.paf.0000163838.92053.fb.

Cambridge Dictionary. "Cultural Appropriation. " *Cambridge University*, https://dictionary.cambridge.org/dictionary/english/cultural-appropriation. Accessed 23 June 2024.

Clemens, Tessa et al. "A Population Based Study of Drowning in Canada." *BMC Public Health*, vol. 16, no. 1, 2016, p. 559.

Coalition for Bereaved Workers. "Statutory Bereavement Leave and Pay in Northern Ireland—A Call to Action." *Marie Curie*, https://www.mariecurie.org.uk/globalassets/media/documents/how-we-can-help/statutory-bereavement-leave-and-pay-in-ni-a-call-to-action.pdf. Accessed 17 June 2024.

"Code of Conduct." *College of Nurses of Ontario*. 2019, https://www.cno.org/globalassets/docs/prac/49040_code-of-conduct.pdf. Accessed 17 June 2024.

"Code of Ethics." *National Association of Social Workers*, 2017, https://www.socialworkers.org/About/Ethics/Code-of-Ethics. Accessed 17 June 2024.

"Coronavirus Tracker." *Worldometer*, 13 Apr. 2024, https://www.worldometers.info/coronavirus/coronavirus-death-toll/. Accessed 17 June 2024.

Cosgrove, Lisa, and Sheldon Krimsky. "A Comparison of DSM-IV and DSM-5 Panel Members' Financial Associations with Industry: A Pernicious Problem Persists." *PLoS Medicine*, vol. 9, no. 3, 2012, pp. e1001190–e1001190.

Dawkins, Richard. *Unweaving the Rainbow: Science, Delusion and the Appetite for Wonder*. Penguin, 1998. http://archive.org/details/unweavingrainbow0000dawk_b8u8.

Dernoot Lipsky Van, Laura, and Connie Burk. *Trauma Stewardship*. Berrett-Koehler Publishers, 2009.

Devine, Megan. *It's OK That You're Not OK: Meeting Grief and Loss in a Culture That Doesn't Understand.* Sounds True, 2017.

Diagnostic and Statistical Manual of Mental Disorders: DSM-5-TR. 5th ed. American Psychiatric Association Publishing, 2022.

Doka, Kenneth J., editor. *Disenfranchised Grief: Recognizing Hidden Sorrow.* Lexington Books/D. C. Heath and Com, 1989.

Doka, Kenneth J. *Disenfranchised Grief: New Directions, Challenges, and Strategies for Practice.* Research Press, 2002.

Doka, Kenneth J., and Terry Martin. Grieving Beyond Gender: Understanding the Ways Men and Women Mourn. Routledge, 2011.

Doubek, Kelly and James Doubek. "Psychologist On Why Funerals Are Fundamental to Processing Grief." *NPR—All Things Considered.* NPR, 14 Dec. 2020, https://www.npr.org/sections/coronavirus-live-updates/2020/12/14/946402101/psychologist-on-why-funerals-are-fundamental-to-processing-grief. Accessed 17 June 2024.

Drummond-Smith, Flora, and Chris Saunders. "Photo Story: Pantsula Dance in Johannesburg." *Aston Martin Magazine,* https://magazine.astonmartin.com/travel/photo-story-pantsula-dance-johannesburg-chris-saunders. Accessed 17 June 2024.

Dunbar, R.I.M. "The Social Brain: Psychological Underpinnings and Implications for the Structure of Organizations." *Current Directions in Psychological Science* 23, no. 2, 2014, pp. 109–14.

Eromosele, Aimaloghi. "There Is No Self-Care without Community Care." *URGE,* 2020, https://urge.org/there-is-no-self-care-without-community-care/. Accessed 17 June 2024.

Ethans, Paula. "Every Self for Themselves." *Kaur Space,* 2019, https://kaurspace.com/magazine/13/self-for-themselves-paula-ethan. Accessed 17 June 2024.

Fagundes, Christopher P., et al. "Grief, Depressive Symptoms, and Inflammation in the Spousally Bereaved." *Psychoneuroendocrinology,* vol. 100, Feb. 2019, pp. 190–97. *ScienceDirect,* https://doi.org/10.1016/j.psyneuen.2018.10.006.

Fernández-Alcántara, Manuel, et al. "Assessment of different components of executive function in grief | Psicothema." *Psicotherma,* vol. 28, no. 3, May 2016, pp. 260–65. *reunido.uniovi.es,* https://doi.org/10.7334/psicothema2015.257.

Freed, Peter J., et al. "Neural Mechanisms of Grief Regulation." *Biological Psychiatry*, vol. 66, no. 1, July 2009, pp. 33–40. *www.biologicalpsychiatryjournal.com*, https://doi.org/10.1016/j.biopsych.2009.01.019.

Gang, James, et al. "Naltrexone Treatment for Prolonged Grief Disorder: Study Protocol for a Randomized, Triple-Blinded, Placebo-Controlled Trial." *Current Controlled Trials in Cardiovascular Medicine*, vol. 22, no. 1, 2021, p. 110.

Glass Door. "Nurse Salary in Canada." *Glass Door*, https://www.glassdoor.ca/Salaries/nurse-salary-SRCH_KO0,5.htm. Accessed 17 June 2024.

Glass Door. "Social Worker Salary in Canada." *Glass Door*, https://www.glassdoor.ca/Salaries/social-worker-salary-SRCH_KO0,13.htm. Accessed 17 June 2024.

Hairston, Stephanie. "How Grief Shows Up In Your Body." *WebMD*, https://www.webmd.com/special-reports/grief-stages/20190711/how-grief-affects-your-body-and-mind. Accessed 17 June 2024.

Hedayat, Kamyar M. "The Theory of Endobiogeny: Biological Modeling Using Downstream Physiologic Output as Inference of Upstream Global System Regulation." *Journal of Complexity in Health Sciences*, vol. 3, no. 1, 1, June 2020, pp. 1–8. *www.extrica.com*, https://doi.org/10.21595/chs.2020.21072.

Hicks, Angela M., and Carolyn Korbel. "Attachment Theory." *Encyclopedia of Behavioral Medicine*. Edited by Marc D. Gellman and J. Rick Turner, Springer, 2013, pp. 149–55, https://doi.org/10.1007/978-1-4419-1005-9_939.

Hospice Palliative Care Ontario. *2020–2021 Annual Report*. HPCO, 2022.

Houska, Tara. "Houska: 'I Didn't Know' Doesn't Cut It Anymore." *Indian Country Today*, 16 Apr. 2015, http://indiancountrytodaymedianetwork.com/2015/04/16/houska-i-didnt-know-doesnt-cut-it-anymore-160051. Accessed 17 June 2024.

Hurley, Katie. "Helping Preschoolers Cope with Separation Anxiety." *PBS*, 2015, https://www.pbs.org/parents/thrive/helping-preschoolers-cope-with-separation-anxiety. Accessed 17 Oct. 2024.

Janoff-Bulman, Ronnie. "Assumptive Worlds and the Stress of Traumatic Events: Applications of the Schema Construct." *Social Cognition* 7, no. 2, 1989, pp. 113–36. https://doi.org/10.1521/soco.1989.7.2.113.

Johnson, Kjerstin. "Don't Mess Up When You Dress Up: Cultural Appropriation and Costumes." *Bitch Magazine*, 25 Oct. 2011, https://bitchmedia.org/post/costume-cultural-appropriation. Accessed 23 June 2023.

Kaufman-Mthimkhulu, Stefanie Lyn. "Why Prolonged Grief Shouldn't Be Considered a Mental Illness—Especially During a Pandemic." *well+good*, 5 June 2022. https://www.wellandgood.com/prolonged-grief/. Accessed 17 June 2024.

KidsHealth. "The Importance of Attachment in Babies." *KidsHealth*, Pediatric Society of New Zealand, https://www.kidshealth.org.nz/importance-attachment-babies. Accessed 17 June 2024.

Kübler-Ross, Elisabeth. "On Death and Dying: A Reappraisal." *Mortality*, vol. 18, no. 1, pp. 94–97. DOI: 10.1080/13576275.2012.758629

Labbé, Stefan. "Canadian Women Do 50% More Unpaid Housework than Men, Finds StatsCan." *Times Colonist*, 18 Mar. 2022, https://www.timescolonist.com/life/canadian-women-do-50-more-unpaid-housework-than-men-finds-stats-can-5172421. Accessed 17 June 2024.

Levy-Ward, Anne. "How Much Does a Funeral Cost? | Sun Life Canada." *SunLife*, https://www.sunlife.ca/en/insurance/life/how-much-does-a-funeral-cost/. Accessed 17 June 2024.

LeWine, Howard. "Takotsubo Cardiomyopathy (Broken-Heart Syndrome)." *Harvard Health*, 20, Oct. 2010, https://www.health.harvard.edu/heart-health/takotsubo-cardiomyopathy-broken-heart-syndrome. Accessed 17 June 2024.

"Licensed Social Worker Demographics and Statistics in the Us." *Zippia*, 2022, https://www.zippia.com/licensed-social-worker-jobs/demographics/. Accessed 17 June 2024.

Lorde, Audre. "A Burst of Light and Other Essays." Firebrand Books, 1988.

"Male Nursing Statistics 2022–2023, 2021–2020." *AB Staffing Solutions*, 2022, https://www.abstaffing.com/male-nursing-statistics/. Accessed 17 June 2024.

Maxouris, Christina, and Hollie Silverman. "Atatiana Jefferson's Father Dies Weeks after His Daughter Was Killed by a Police Officer." *CNN*, 2019. https://edition.cnn.com/2019/11/09/us/atatiana-jefferson-father-dies/index.html. Accessed 17 June 2024.

McVean, Ada. "It's Time to Let the Five Stages of Grief Die." *McGill University*, 2019, https://www.mcgill.ca/oss/article/health-history/its-time-let-five-stages-grief-die. Accessed 17 June 2024.

Mills, Mary Alice. *Shattered Assumptions? A Prospective Study: The Impact of Trauma on Global Beliefs and Adjustment*. ProQuest, 2010, https://www.proquest.com/docview/858608633.

Miserandino, Christine. “The Spoon Theory.” *But You Don’t Look Sick?*, 25 Apr. 2013, https://butyoudontlooksick.com/articles/written-by-christine/the-spoon-theory/. Accessed 17 June 2024.

Mostofsky, Elizabeth, et al. “Risk of Acute Myocardial Infarction After the Death of a Significant Person in One’s Life.” *Circulation*, vol. 125, no. 3, Jan. 2012, pp. 491–96. *ahajournals.org (Atypon)*, https://doi.org/10.1161/CIRCULATION AHA.111.061770.

Nabili, Siamak. “Facts About the History of Hospice and Respite Care.” *MedicineNet*, https://www.medicinenet.com/hospice/article.htm#hospice_facts. Accessed 17 June 2024.

“Naltrexone HCL Market Growth 2023-2030.” *Precision Reports*, 2023, https://www.linkedin.com/pulse/naltrexone-hcl-market-growth-2023-2030-92-pages/. Accessed 17 June 2024.

National Council for Palliative Care (NCPC). “Life after Death: Six Steps to Support in Bereavement.” *NCPC*, https://hospiceuk-files-prod.s3.eu-west-2.amazonaws.com/s3fs-public/2022-11/life-after-death-bereavement-report.pdf. Accessed 23 June 2024.

NBC News. “Family Speaks for First Time Since Atatiana Jefferson’s Mother’s Death.” *NBC 5 Dallas-Fort Worth*, 9 Jan. 2020, https://www.nbcdfw.com/news/local/mother-dies-months-after-her-daughter-atatiana-jefferson-killed-in-house-by-fort-worth-officer/2289321/. Accessed 17 June 2024.

NCPC. “Bereaved People Being Failed by Lack of Support in the Workplace.” *NCPC*, https://www.ncpc.org.uk/news/bereaved-people-being-failed-lack-support-workplace. Accessed 17 June 2024.

O’Connor, Mary-Frances. “Immunological and Neuroimaging Biomarkers of Complicated Grief.” *Dialogues in Clinical Neuroscience*, vol. 14, no. 2, June 2012, pp. 141–48.

Osterweis, Marian, et al., editors. “Toward a Biology of Grieving.” *Bereavement: Reactions, Consequences, and Care*. National Academies Press (US), 1984, www.ncbi.nlm.nih.gov, https://www.ncbi.nlm.nih.gov/books/NBK217841/.

Owen, Jessica. “Cremation More Popular than Burial, Says Local Funeral Director.” *Collingwood Today*, 15 Mar. 2023, https://www.collingwoodtoday.ca/local-news/cremation-more-popular-than-burial-says-local-funeral-director-6702435. Accessed 17 June 2024.

Parkes, C. Murray. "What Becomes of Redundant World Models? A Contribution to the Study of Adaptation to Change." *British Journal of Medical Psychology* 48, no. 2 (1975): 131–37. https://doi.org/10.1111/j.2044-8341.1975.tb02315.x.

Perreault, Charles, and Sarah Mathew. "Dating the Origin of Language Using Phonemic Diversity." *PloS One*, vol. 7, no. 4, 2012, pp. e35289–e35289.

Phillips, Anna C., et al. "Bereavement and Marriage Are Associated with Antibody Response to Influenza Vaccination in the Elderly." *Brain, Behavior, and Immunity*, vol. 20, no. 3, May 2006, pp. 279–89. *PubMed*, https://doi.org/10.1016/j.bbi.2005.08.003.

Porteous-Sebouhian, Bryony. "Why acknowledging and celebrating the Black feminist origins of 'self-care' Is essential." *Mental Health Today*, 2021, https://www.mentalhealthtoday.co.uk/blog/awareness/why-acknowledging-and-celebrating-the-black-feminist-origins-of-self-care-is-essential. Accessed 17 June 2024.

"Respecting and Supporting Grief at Work: How Employers Can Better Support Their Staff through Personal Loss." *Marie Curie*, https://www.mariecurie.org.uk/globalassets/media/documents/how-we-can-help/bereavement-hub/respecting-and-supporting-grief-at-work_sep-2021.pdf. Accessed 17 June 2024.

Rogers, Richard A. "From Cultural Exchange to Transculturation: A Review and Reconceptualization of Cultural Appropriation." *Communication Theory*, vol. 16, no. 4, Nov. 2006, pp. 474–503. *Silverchair*, https://doi.org/10.1111/j.1468-2885.2006.00277.x.

Schneck, Noam, Tao Tu, Christina A. Michel, et al. "Attentional Bias to Reminders of the Deceased as Compared with a Living Attachment in Grieving." *Biological Psychiatry: Cognitive Neuroscience and Neuroimaging*, vol. 3, no. 2, Feb. 2018, pp. 107–15. *ScienceDirect*, https://doi.org/10.1016/j.bpsc.2017.08.003.

Schneck, Noam, Tao Tu, Stefan Haufe, et al. "Ongoing Monitoring of Mindwandering in Avoidant Grief through Cortico-Basal-Ganglia Interactions." *Social Cognitive and Affective Neuroscience*, vol. 14, no. 2, Feb. 2019, pp. 163–72. *Silverchair*, https://doi.org/10.1093/scan/nsy114.

Schuurman, Donna. "The Grief Pill is Coming!" *Mad in America*, 5 Apr. 2022, https://www.madinamerica.com/2022/04/grief-pill-coming/. Accessed 17 June 2024.

Silva, Adriana C., et al. "Neurological Aspects of Grief." *CNS & Neurological Disorders Drug Targets*, vol. 13, no. 6, 2014, pp. 930–36. *PubMed*, https://doi.org/10.2174/1871527313666140612120018.

Society for Human Resource Management. "Survey." *SHRM*, 2020, https://shrm-res.cloudinary.com/image/upload/v1630503564/2020%20Employee%20Benefits/Benefits_Full_Report_FINAL_1.pdf. Accessed 17 June 2024.

Solomon, Samson. "Canada Housing Market | 2024 Home Prices." *Nesto*, 15 May 2024, https://www.nesto.ca/real-estate/canadian-housing-market-outlook/. Accessed 17 June 2024.

St. Christopher's Hospice. "Our History: Dame Cicely Saunders." *St Christopher's*, https://www.stchristophers.org.uk/about/damecicelysaunders. Accessed 17 June 2024.

Statistics Canada. "Average Weekly Working Hours, 1976 to 2022." *Statistics Canada*, Government of Canada, 13 June 2023, https://www150.statcan.gc.ca/n1/pub/14-28-0001/2023001/article/00001-eng.htm. Accessed 17 June 2024.

Strayed, Cheryl. "The Love of My Life." *The Sun Magazine*, Oct. 2023, https://www.thesunmagazine.org/issues/574/the-love-of-my-life-issue-574. Accessed 17 June 2024.

Stroebe, M., et al. "Cautioning Health-Care Professionals." *Omega*, vol. 74, no. 4, pp. 455–73.

The Canadian Encyclopedia. "The Krever Inquiry." *The Canadian Encyclopedia*, https://www.thecanadianencyclopedia.ca/en/article/krever-inquiry. Accessed 17 June 2024.

"The U.S. Mental Health Market: $225.1 Billion In Spending In 2019: An OPEN MINDS Market Intelligence Report." *OpenMinds*, 2020. https://openminds.com/intelligence-report/the-u-s-mental-health-market-225-1-billion-in-spending-in-2019-an-open-minds-market-intelligence-report/. Accessed 17 June 2024.

Toop, Chrystal Waban. "Reclaiming Cultural Teachings about Mortality, Grief, Loss, Death and Dying." *Dying with Dignity*, 17 June 2022, https://www.dyingwithdignity.ca/blog/reclaiming-cultural-teachings-about-mortality-grief-loss-death-and-dying/. Accessed 17 June 2024.

United Nations Educational, Scientific and Cultural Organization. "Decorated Cave of Pont d'Arc, Known as Grotte Chauvet-Pont d'Arc, Ardèche." *UNESCO*, 2014, https://whc.unesco.org/en/list/1426. Accessed 17 June 2025.

Vitlic, Ana, et al. "Bereavement Reduces Neutrophil Oxidative Burst Only in Older Adults: Role of the HPA Axis and Immunesenescence." *Immunity & Ageing*, vol. 11, no. 1, Aug. 2014, p. 13. *BioMed Central*, https://doi.org/10.1186/1742-4933-11-13.

Walker, Andy. "Eirene: Report Reveals Many Canadians Would Struggle with the Cost of a Funeral." *Eirene*, https://eirenecremations.com/blog/angus-reid-report-many-canadians-would-struggle-with-funeral-cost. Accessed 17 June 2024.

Watson, Laurie J. "Why and How to Talk About Sex While Grieving." *Psychology Today*, Accessed May 22, 2024. https://www.psychologytoday.com/us/blog/married-and-still-doing-it/202108/why-and-how-talk-about-sex-while-grieving. Accessed 17 June 2024.

Watson, Laurie J., and George Faller. *Episode 295: How To Talk About Sex While Grieving—Foreplay Radio—Couples and Sex Therapy*. Podcast, 2021. https://www.foreplayrst.com/how-to-talk-about-sex-while-grieving/. Accessed 17 June 2024.

Weiss, Robert. *Loneliness: The Experience of Emotional and Social Isolation*. The MIT Press, 1975.

Wikipedia. "Cultural Appropriation." *Wikipedia*, https://en.wikipedia.org/wiki/Cultural_appropriation. Accessed 23 June 2024.

Wolfe, Blake. "A Look at Current Provincial Policies on Bereavement Leave." *Benefits Canada*, 16 Sept. 2021, https://www.benefitscanada.com/benefits/absence-management/a-look-at-current-provincial-policies-on-bereavement-leave/. Accessed 17 June 2024.

Zaslow, Jeffrey. "New Index Aims to Calculate the Annual Cost of Despair." *Wall Street Journal*, 20 Nov. 2002, https://www.wsj.com/articles/SB103773937895627388. Accessed 17 June 2024.

About the Author

Rachelle Bensoussan holds a master's degree in Thanatology and has spent the last fifteen years advancing grief literacy across Canada and the United States. She is a former faculty member at both McMaster University's Michael G. DeGroote School of Medicine and King's University College. Rachelle is a two-time nominee for the Association of Death Education and Counselling's Academic Educator Award and Community Educator Award. Rachelle is a Queer woman of North-African & Middle Eastern descent. She currently lives in Toronto with her brilliant wife, her magical daughter, and her highly dysregulated Yorkshire Terrier. You can learn more about Rachelle and her work at: www.griefliteracy.ca

Deepest appreciation to
Demeter's monthly Donors

DEMETER

Daughters

Brent & Heather Beal
Carole Trainor
Khin May Kyawt
Tatjana Takseva
Debbie Byrd
Tanya Cassidy
Myrel Chernick
Marcella Gemelli
Donna Lee, In Memory of Dee Stark, RN, LNHA,
Trailblazer for Women, Women's Rights Advocate
Catherine Cheleen-Mosqueda

Sisters

Fiona Green
Paul Chu
Amber Kinser
Nicole Willey

Mother

Mildred Bennett Walker (Trainor)

Grandmother

Tina Powell